Memory and Narrative at the Origin of the Novel

This book investigates certain recurrent structures in the history of the novel as a textual genre and as a narrative form typical of Western literature. From its origins, in the vernacular cultures of the twelfth and thirteenth centuries, the novel text seems to be characterised by certain stylistic procedures adopted to represent a new narrative framework, which has no direct terms of comparison in the previous literary tradition. Indeed, the novel, as a 'textual machine', often produces a 'narrative manipulation' of time and duration, to the point of establishing, along its development, a very close link between History, individual memory and a prospective narrative future. This book explores some structural and formal paths of the 'novelistic machine', through three exemplary cases: (1) the 'name of the novel' at the origins of the literary genre, with the invention of a new 'novelistic technique' (i.e. the *conjointure*) by Chrétien de Troyes (twelfth century); (2) the book-form, namely, 'the book of novels' as a concrete and material object that transmits the narrative text and involves itself within the fictional universe; (3) the literary topos of the 'dreaming incipit' and its long history from the *Roman de la rose* to Proust. This book will be of significant interest to students and scholars of medieval literature, the history of the novel and philology.

Lorenzo Mainini is lecturer in Romance Philology at Sapienza University of Rome, Italy.

Young Feltrinelli Prize in the Moral Sciences
Roberto Antonelli, *President, Class of Moral Sciences, Accademia Nazionale dei Lincei*
Alberto Quadrio Curzio, *President Emeritus, Accademia Nazionale dei Lincei*
Alessandro Roncaglia, *Joint Academic Administrator, Accademia Nazionale dei Lincei*

The Accademia Nazionale dei Lincei, founded in 1603, is one of the oldest academies in the world. Since 2018, it has awarded four Young Antonio Feltrinelli Prizes every two years, to Italian researchers in the fields of moral sciences and humanities who are younger than 40 years old. Each winner is then requested to write a book-length essay on their research and/or the perspectives of research in their field, directed to the general public. The Routledge Young Feltrinelli Prize in the Moral Sciences series thus includes high-quality essays by top young researchers, providing thoroughly readable contributions to different research fields. With this initiative, Accademia dei Lincei not only gives a remarkable grant to the winners of the prize in order to support their research activity, but also contributes to the international diffusion of the research of eminent young Italian scholars.

Petrarch and Boccaccio in the First Commentaries on Dante's *Commedia*
A Literary Canon before Its Official Birth
Luca Fiorentini

Pliny the Elder and the Matter of Memory
An Encyclopaedic Workshop
Anna Anguissola

Memory and Narrative at the Origin of the Novel
Three studies, from Chrétien de Troyes to Proust
Lorenzo Mainini

For more information about this series, please visit: www.routledge.com/Young-Feltrinelli-Prize-in-the-Moral-Sciences/book-series/YFP

Memory and Narrative at the Origin of the Novel
Three studies, from Chrétien de Troyes to Proust

Lorenzo Mainini

LONDON AND NEW YORK

Revision of English text by Richard Bates

First published 2024
by Routledge
4 Park Square, Milton Park, Abingdon, Oxon OX14 4RN

and by Routledge
605 Third Avenue, New York, NY 10158

Routledge is an imprint of the Taylor & Francis Group, an informa business

© 2024 Lorenzo Mainini

The right of Lorenzo Mainini to be identified as author of this work has been asserted in accordance with sections 77 and 78 of the Copyright, Designs and Patents Act 1988.

All rights reserved. No part of this book may be reprinted or reproduced or utilised in any form or by any electronic, mechanical, or other means, now known or hereafter invented, including photocopying and recording, or in any information storage or retrieval system, without permission in writing from the publishers.

Trademark notice: Product or corporate names may be trademarks or registered trademarks, and are used only for identification and explanation without intent to infringe.

British Library Cataloguing-in-Publication Data
A catalogue record for this book is available from the British Library

ISBN: 978-1-032-12222-9 (hbk)
ISBN: 978-1-032-12223-6 (pbk)
ISBN: 978-1-003-22364-1 (ebk)

DOI: 10.4324/9781003223641

Typeset in Times New Roman
by Newgen Publishing UK

Contents

Foreword   *vi*

1   *Conjointure*
Chrétien de Troyes, Servius and the
Virgilian tradition   1

2   Books of stories and books of novels   36

3   Dreaming the incipit (towards Proust
and the *Rose*)   68

Index   *110*

Foreword

This book brings together three studies on the novel, from a dual perspective: the novel as a literary genre with a long history and, at the same time, the novel as a textual form with its own specific narrative language. While, on the surface, the three studies display their own critical autonomy (i.e. each one examines a particular issue of the novel genre), the internal links between the three chapters make these studies parts of a single discourse. Their mutual coherence lies in the following theme: at its origin in the second half of the twelfth century – when the first narrative works appeared in vernacular languages –, the novel text faced the problem of its structural unity. What unifies the parts of a story? What expressive devices does the text use to organise the unity of its narrative? The search for an answer to these questions will focus on the medieval literary tradition and then draw comparative observations with the narrative language of the modern novel as a whole.

As a literary genre, the novel has no direct antecedents in classical Greek and Latin literature.[1] Its modern structure aims to establish a substantial isomorphism between the 'unity of narrative' and the 'unity of subjective experience'. In other words, the diegetic plane of the narrative seeks to simulate a relationship with the experience of the events represented in the text. For this purpose, the novel adopts some stylistic procedures to manipulate time and duration in order to deal effectively with diegetic fragmentation. In particular, the novel's narrative devices seem to operate at the intersection of History, individual memory and future narrative perspectives as the storyline develops.

Therefore, ever since its medieval origins, the novel has had to resolve, on the level of textual fiction, the problem of the unity of experience, embodied in the identity of the fictional character, and that of its diegetic representation, which, conversely, may entail on the level of writing the effects of fragmentation in composition, language and memory. The resulting work is thus the outcome of two distinct forces: on the one hand, the ordering and unifying force inherent in any text and, on the other, the episodic and multiple aspect of the lives and existential circumstances reflected in the narrative. The novel, in this sense, is a diegetic and linguistic exercise on time and, in particular, on duration: the text stands as a connecting centre between the occurrence of the narrated facts, the memory of them in the narrating subject, and their future in the writing.

It is by virtue of this internal structure, operating between fiction and experience – memory and future – that the novel has been able to become the 'pedagogical genre' of modern literature: the 'moral book' that shows and teaches human behaviour in the duration of experience. Moreover, it is by virtue of this very structure that the novel gradually established itself as the 'classical genre' of modernity. Indeed, it offers the moderns' answer to those problems that already defined the core of Aristotelian poetics. For the ancients, the question of unity was resolved through the 'extrinsic' unity of action – unity of time and space; for the moderns, the solution gradually led towards the 'intrinsic' unity of memorial experience. Though this 'intrinsic' unity can override the classical unity of space and time, it cannot renounce some form of subjective unity, even the slimmest – a 'voice', for example, disjointed in the duration of multiple spaces and multiple times.

The three chapters address these issues from three different points of view: (1) research of the sources and the history of tradition; (2) narrative textuality and its repercussions on the novel as a book-object; (3) interdiscoursivity and the making of a memory within the literary genre.

Chapter 1 attempts a new analysis of *conjointure*, that is, the technical term used by Chrétien de Troyes, the greatest twelfth-century narrator, in his first novel, *Erec et Enide*. With that word, or rather with the entire syntagma – *mout bele conjointure*, a 'very beautiful conjunction' –, the poet wanted to define the internal structuring of the story he narrated. *Conjointure* is, in short, the first technical name for the 'novel'. This chapter will show that the notion of *conjointure* comes from the tradition of Virgilian exegesis, in particular from Servius (fourth–fifth century), the author of a fundamental commentary on the *Aeneid*. In his exegesis, Servius formulates the concept of *optima coniunctio* ('perfect conjunction') to explain the articulation of stylistic levels and narrative plots in the Latin poem. The Virgilian *coniunctio* in the *Aeneid* – *optima*, as the *conjointure* is *mout bele* – is the textual device that allows the author, as in Chrétien's novel, to keep together ('to conjoin') parts of narration that differ regarding space and time, or in the subject of the discourse and memory.

Chapter 2, 'Books of stories and books of novels', deals with the relationship between the novel text and the book-object that contains it. At first, we will observe in the medieval manuscript tradition the emergence of a particular book-form that characterises the transmission of narrative texts; starting from these preliminary remarks, we will examine the function of the book as 'objective image' reflected within the novel text. What does a 'book of novels' look like? And how can the novel text internalise its book-object and involve it in narrative fiction? Looking for an answer to such questions, we will explore how the relationship between the text and its book mirrors a prior relationship between the fiction *inside* the novel and the multiplicity of stories and events that remain *outside* the text. In this sense, we interpret the composition of the novel's book as an exercise in unifying different stories and times, that is, an exercise in including an external otherness in the book.

Finally, Chapter 3, 'Dreaming the incipit', is mainly comparative. It observes the recurrence of a topos in the long tradition of the novel genre: this topos concerns the beginning of the narration in a context of oneiric or semi-oneiric recollection. The 'dream of the incipit' can thus be investigated throughout modern literary history. It is, moreover, significant that this 'oneiric typology' occurs at two extreme points of literary chronology, namely, at the origin and at the end of the narrative tradition. Symbolically, we can follow its traces from the thirteenth-century *Roman de la rose* to Proust's *Recherche*. From 'Maintes genz dient qu'en songe / n'ait se fable non et mençonge' ('Many people say that dreams are only fables and lies', *Rose*) to 'Longtemps je me suis couché de bonne heure' ('For a long time I went to bed early', *Recherche*). By virtue of this long tradition, we can discern in the topos a formal solution that can recompose, on a textual level, the fragmented experience in the story and the unity of memory in the narrating subject. Therefore, the 'dreaming incipit', as a strategic narrative device, is actually a textual junction useful for structuring the dialectic between 'variety' and 'unity' that typifies, as a whole, the novel genre.

A final clarification. These chapters deal with the novel as a historical object and as a textual form. That is, they propose, at the same time, historical-diachronic investigations – aimed above all at some issues of the medieval narrative – and synchronic-comparative arguments – that is, some systematic considerations on the novel form, including its development in modern literature. Indeed, we believe that the novel is, to a certain extent, an 'ecological structure'[2] of the tradition and therefore it re-proposes throughout its history some synchronicities and continuities that distinguish the text itself – that is, the novel as a 'narrative language' – as much in the medieval narrative as in the modern novel. This clarification is perhaps pleonastic: the choice of comparing different literary epochs is justified at a theoretical level in some emblematic examples of philological studies – from Erich Auerbach to Ernst Robert Curtius. If we repeat this assumption, it is because these chapters are a philologist's contribution to the study of the novel: that is, they are preliminarily a hermeneutics of tradition. As such, this work can have its own specific value only if its object – the novel text – discloses the structuring dialectic between the 'acts of language', that is, the synchronicity of narrative functions, and its particular 'discourses', that is, the texts individually produced in the course of literary history[3].

Notes

1 Auerbach (1953) discussed 'what classical literature does not possess', compared to the expressive possibilities of 'modern Realism'.
2 Cf. Fuksas 2008, 9: 'assuming such an ecological perspective, [...] the novel [aims] at finding an effective-enough solution to the crucial problem of developing representational schemes'.
3 We are referring to the categories formalised, in the context of Romance philology, by Lausberg (1963, 30) clearly based on Ferdinand de Saussure's assumptions.

References

E. Auerbach, "Epilegomena zu Mimesis", *Romanische Forschungen*, 65 (1953), pp. 1–18.

A.P. Fuksas, "The Embodied Novel", *Cognitive Philology*, 1 (2008), pp. 1–14.

H. Lausberg, *Romanische Sprachwissenschaft*, I, *Einleitung und Vokalismus*, Berlin, De Gruyter, 1963.

1 Conjointure
Chrétien de Troyes, Servius and the Virgilian tradition

The so-called *Tractatus coislinianus*[1] lists among the causes of laughter (γίνεται δὲ ὁ γέλως) – and thus among the various traits of comic *mimesis* – the fact that a story is ἀσυνάρτητος, 'disconnected', 'lacking correspondence between its parts': ὅταν ἀσυνάρτητος ὁ λόγος ᾖ καὶ μηδεμίαν ἀκολουθίαν ἔχων. Earlier, the anonymous author of the *Tractatus* had already argued that the comic effect is attained ἐκ τοῦ δυνατοῦ καὶ ἀνακολούθου, 'because of the possible and the inconsequent', that is, as the result of something that could happen but nevertheless does not follow from its premises – and may indeed disregard them. Laughter in this sense will be the outcome of the unexpected and the contrary. In line with this rhetorical culture, Cicero stated (*De oratore* II, 281 and II, 255): *ridentur etiam discrepantia*, 'we finally laugh for the contradictions'; *notissimum ridiculi genus, cum aliud exspectamus, aliud dicitur*, 'the most notorious kind of ridicule: when we expect something and something else is expressed'. The 'disconnection' or, in the lexicon of *Coislinianus*, the anacoluthon, which is normally counted among the rhetorical figures of the sentence – thus operating on the microscopic level of verbal syntax – is at the same time a macroscopic figure of narrative and dramaturgical syntax. That is, it not only pertains to the word but also to the diegetic structure, to the order of the narrated facts, ἀπὸ τῶν πραγμάτων – according to the *Tractatus*. Therefore, 'comic anacoluthon' occurs when certain actions of the story are not consequential to each other, when certain events of the diegesis are somehow disjointed, unexpected or unrelated.

Whatever the origin of this short Greek compendium – whether from within the early Aristotelian school or a late composition – its interest is assured by the fact that the categories employed are

DOI: 10.4324/9781003223641-1

2 Conjointure

continuous with the tradition of classical poetics. The diegetic anacoluthon – that is, the fragmentation, disconnection and disjunction of narrative parts – is indeed a theoretical and stylistic form linked to the background of other Aristotelian conceptions. Firstly, of course, the notion of unity: a 'single fact' (μίαν πρᾶξιν, *Poetics* 7, 1451a 25); secondly, the notion of extension (μέγεθος ἐχούσης, *Poetics* 5, 1449b 25), both of which denote the idea of the tragic in Aristotle, for whom tragedy is a work that represents a single action within the same narrative extension that coordinates its parts. The relationship between the parts of the single tragic action will also be perfect if the facts of the story, however surprising, appear consequential to each other by virtue of some necessity, ἐπίτηδες (*Poetics* 9, 1452a 5–10). It would seem, therefore, that the tragic effect is produced by the unity of the parts and the 'causal' coherence of their relationship – by destiny and necessity: that is, by means opposite to some forms of the 'comic plot' listed in *Coislinianus* – 'disconnection' and non-correspondence.

In the second half of the twelfth century in France, the question – without any direct influence from the ancient Greek problem – reappeared in comparable forms in the work of Chrétien de Troyes, in the course of the prologue to *Erec et Enide* (vv. 9–26).[2]

Por ce dit Crestiiens de Troies
que reisons est que totes voies
doit chascuns panser et antandre
a bien dire et a bien aprandre,
et tret d'un conte d'avanture
une mout bele conjointure,
par qu'an puet prover et savoir
que cil ne fet mie savoir,
qui sa sciance n'abandone
tant con Deus la grace l'an done.
D'Erec, le fil Lac, est li contes,
que devant rois et devant contes
depecier et *corronpre* suelent
cil qui de conter vivre vuelent.
Des or comancerai l'estoire
qui toz jorz mes iert an memoire
tant con durra crestiantez;
de ce s'est Crestiiens vantez.

[Then, Chrétien de Troyes says that it is right to always think and devote oneself to telling well and teaching well; *and he draws from a tale of adventure a beautiful conjuncture*, through which one can verify and know that he is not at all wise who does not spread his knowledge – as God has given him grace. The story is that of Erec, son of Lac, which is usually *fragmented and broken up* by those who make their living telling tales at the courts of kings and counts. Now I will start the story that will remain in memory forever, as long as Christianity exists – this is Chrétien's boast].

Critics have discussed these verses extensively, seeking to explain certain programmatic expressions contained therein. The object of their research is obviously the meaning of *conjointure*, which in Chrétien's lexicon seems to name the outcome of his new *modus narrandi*, the entire poetic operation developed in the text. From a previous tale of adventure (*conte d'avanture*) – we read in the prologue – the poet has elaborated a 'beautiful conjuncture', which will therefore be the authentic form of the novel, distinct from its 'source', that is, the *conte d'avanture* from which the novel derives. The notion of *conjointure* – the novel as 'conjunction' – brings to mind, as was already the case in *Coislinianus*, the themes of narrative unity and diegetic parts and their relationship – connective or disjunctive;[3] in short, the question of 'novelistic montage'. The same issues – the unity and conjunction between the parts – reappear in the following lines, where Chrétien criticises *cil qui de conter vivre vuelent*, that is, the jesters and professional storytellers. According to Chrétien, they are guilty of *depecier* and *corronpre*, that is, of 'dismembering' the unity of the fictional *conjointure*.

The passage from the *Erec* is also one of the most symbolic texts for the development of the modern novel. In its lines, we can discern the first self-conscious reflection of the novel as a literary genre that was destined to impose itself on Western literary culture. After the phase of the so-called narratives of ancient matter, inspired by or translated from sources of classical historiography and epic (*Roman de Troie*, *Eneas*, *Roman de Thèbes* and the works of Wace),[4] Chrétien's novel, dating from around 1170, is situated precisely at the origin of the literary genre.[5] With the *Erec* we are therefore at the origins of a new narrative language, of its autonomous poetic constitution. Perhaps it was for these reasons that Chrétien felt he had to explain and praise ("de ce s'est Crestiiens vantez") the originality of his discovery.

In these pages, I will try a new critical exercise around the *mout bele conjointure*. If the novel at its inception defines, or produces, 'conjuncture', then we shall need to understand why. The rhyme *avanture : conjointure* (vv. 13–14) then confirms the intentionality of the lexical choice, which perhaps indicates an attempt at technicality: a particularly well-considered lexical option aimed at creating a metonymic effect with the meaning of *roman* ('novel'). This lemma in Old French was certainly already well attested in Chrétien's time – the last decades of the twelfth century – but its semantics had not yet been restricted to the mere definition of the literary genre (*roman* = novel/romance). Instead, *roman* retained the possibility of its early, overarching meaning, that is, 'vernacular/romance languages', derived from *romanice loqui*. Thus, the language of expression (*langue romane*) and the literary genre (*roman*) were not yet semantically distinct.[6]

If, therefore, the historical etymology of the literary genre coincided with the birth of Romance literatures (*romanice* > romance) – with the act of storytelling in the vernacular – the lemma *conjointure* might, by contrast, express a poetic and structural definition of the novel, regardless of its vernacular linguistic form.

However, what is the story – the action or the *conjointure* – of *Erec et Enide* about?

The events begin in spring, at Arthur's court. The king wants to revive an ancient custom, the hunting of the white stag, so Arthur and his barons set off into the forest to capture the mythical animal. If the adventure is successful, back at the palace the king will chastely kiss the most beautiful woman in the court. Away from the hunters, with his horse at walking pace, Erec advances into the forest beside Guinevere, the king's wife. Another unknown knight approaches him. This mysterious man offends the queen and one of her handmaidens; he also threatens Erec, attacks him and flees. Erec, shocked, sets out in search of the churlish knight. In his wanderings he reaches a castle; he enters to ask for hospitality. The lord of the castle is courteous, welcomes Erec and introduces him to his wife and daughter. The girl's name is Enide; she seems beautiful to Erec and he would like her for himself.

However, the lord of the castle informs Erec that a knight will appear the next day, to be victorious in a tournament and obtain a sparrowhawk to offer to his beloved. Erec wants to challenge the knight and win the animal so that he can offer it to Enide and ask for her hand in marriage. The knight appears and Erec – as chance would have it – recognises the man who had attacked him the day before. The combat is violent, but Erec is the winner. Enide will then be his wife and will follow him on horseback to Arthur's court. Here, in the meantime, the king and his barons have returned: the white stag has been captured, the custom has been restored, and the king is ready to kiss the most beautiful woman in the court. Erec and Enide make their entrance; the girl receives the king's kiss – she is the most beautiful in the court – and they ask permission to marry. Erec and Enide travel side by side to the court of Erec's father and there they marry. But something happens: the love that binds them to each other is too strong: the couple are found lacking in society, they linger in bed late. Erec is found lacking in his obligations as a knight, he no longer leaves the bedroom. That marriage, the pride of the court, has turned into an exclusive, selfish and antisocial bond. People begin to murmur, mock and blame the couple. One day Enide, eavesdropping on the barons' conversation, learns of the disrepute into which she and her husband have fallen because of their isolated life. She suffers and believes herself guilty. Erec hears her sobbing and, still in the secrecy of their rooms, wants to know the reason for her sudden grief. He too discovers, through his wife, that the court despises their intense bond. The decision follows immediately: Erec sets off on an adventure. Not alone, he takes with him Enide, who is mysteriously obliged to keep silent. With her, he will face a long series of trials, dangers, duels and ambushes, which will have to re-establish the couple's honour. Husband and wife always emerge victorious from their many adventures. There remains the last one: an adventure that everyone fears, called the *Joie de la cour*, 'Joy of the court'. Erec and Enide walk towards a fog-shrouded garden; at its edge Erec leaves his wife and continues alone. In the garden lives a knight, Mabonagrain, with his lady, who rests languidly in the shade of a sycamore tree. The two lovers have lived in isolation for years, satisfied only by their passion, fulfilled only by themselves. The knight Mabonagrain has sworn that he will kill anyone who tries to break their isolated refuge of passion. Erec challenges Mabonagrain and after a bloody duel defeats him. The spell is broken: Mabonagrain and his lady – ghostly doubles of the protagonist couple – come back to real life, and the 'Joy of the court' is restored. Having passed this final adventure, Erec and Enide come back. They have changed, they are mature, they are ready to inherit the kingdom. The story can thus conclude with the crowning of the couple.

This summary can perhaps perform the function of a synopsis, listing some plot stages one after the other, but it certainly does not exhaust the question 'about what?' – which is important for a structural analysis. What is the novel about? This should be answered, as taught by Gérard Genette, with a single proposition, since "tout récit [...] est une production linguistique assumant la relation d'un ou plusieurs événements [...], le développement, aussi monstrueux qu'on voudra, donné à une forme verbale, au sens grammatical du terme: l'expansion d'un verbe."[7] Umberto Eco expressed similar ideas, albeit in a different critical language. If any term includes the totality of information concerning it[8] – 'house', for example, will include, among other aspects, 'foundation', 'masonry', 'bedroom', possibly 'family life', 'childhood' and so on – from a narrative point of view, that term will always entail a preliminary discourse on the *modus operandi* to produce it:[9] that is, the implicit recapitulation, in the mind of the receiver, of all the meanings included in its sign. Eco thus derived from this assumption that the text is an 'expanded sememe',[10] while Genette deduced his *about* of the most complex narrative plots from similar assumptions: the *Odyssey* would be a 'verbal expansion' of the sentence *Ulysses returns to Ithaca* and Proust's *Recherche* a development of the single proposition *Marcel becomes a writer*.[11] From this perspective, the 'basic verb' of Chrétien's novel could then be reduced to the statement "Marriage to Enide risks compromising Erec's life".

Identifying the marriage as the 'narrative verb' is a critical choice that explicitly distances itself from other readings: in particular from those that interpret Chrétien's work in a symbolic-feudal key,[12] focusing on the protagonist's path to the kingdom – with his final coronation – and in the dialectic between courtly and monarchical values. This hypothesis, in my opinion, while ideologically plausible, is nevertheless misleading from a philological and linguistic perspective. Continuing the Proustian comparison, it would be like saying that the 'verb' or the 'sememe' of the

Recherche are the Guermantes, that is, the aristocratic family first coveted by the child, and precluded to him during his sleeplessness and walks in the *overture*, and finally effectively downgraded, during the *matinée* reception that concludes the *Recherche*. Of course, this is not the case. The Guermantes are one of the subjects the narrator's memory takes hold of for a long time; they are the substratum of a process of remembering, which at first spirals, progressing with constant repetitions and involuntary fits and starts. It is only at the end, during that *matinée* at the Guermantes, that this process is resolved, so that Marcel can narrate it and thus 'become a writer'. The 'verbal form' identified by Genette is therefore correct; it is the 'narrative verb', just as 'conjugal danger' is *Erec*'s 'verb'. Indeed, we could specify its enunciation in the even narrower form "Erec becomes a husband".[13] The coronation, or the feudal kingship, on which Chrétien's work closes has, in short, the same narrative values as the *matinée* at the Guermantes. Both constitute the ritual solemnity, or the worldly apotheosis, of the diegetic solution – the event that resolves the narrative circle – but they cannot be confused with generative unity, with the sememe or with the *expansion du verbe*.

The conjugal plot thus structures Chrétien's novel. According to some hypotheses, the marriage of Erec and Enide is so significant that it evolves into a symbolic meaning: on the one hand the narrative marriage of the two protagonists, the 'real' wedding of Erec and Enide; on the other a symbolic *connubium*. This latter would be the true meaning, and the source, of the *conjointure*, as the union, *coniunctio*, of the two characters, endowed with allegorical values: male and female figures of Wisdom, for example,[14] symbolism of which goes beyond the merely compositional and narrative level.[15] In these pages, however, I prefer to give a philological and formal reading of the *conjointure*, leaving aside the symbolism and biblical or clerical allegories included in the marriage plot. The novel will be read primarily as a 'diegetic conjunction'.

Moreover, other passages in Chrétien's work seem to confirm the centrality of the marriage plot as a 'narrative verb'. In the prologue to *Cligès* – his second text according to the author's chronology – Chrétien reminds his readers that he has already composed a novel: "cil qui fist d'Erec et d'Enide" (v. 8),[16] 'the one who already composed the work of Erec and Enide', the title emphasising the double and twofold character – husband and wife – of the first novel. In contrast, in the lines of *Erec*, Chrétien himself, speaking of the jesters who shatter the novelistic *conjointure*, had stated something different. That is, he had distinguished his 'conjugal novel' from those mediocre jesters' tales that narrated only the exploits of the knight – evidently ignoring the 'story of him and her'. "D'Erec, le fil Lac, est li contes, / que devant rois et devant contes / depecier et corronpre suelent / cil qui de conter vivre vuelent", 'the story is that of Erec, son of Lac, which is usually fragmented and broken up by those who make their living telling tales at the courts of kings and counts'. A comparison of the incipit in each of the two texts reveals a clear contrast: there is the 'novel of Erec and Enide', whose title refers to both partners in the marriage, as he reminds us in the prologue to *Cligès*, but there is also the 'tale of Erec alone', fragmented, or badly narrated, by the jesters criticised in the first work.

The novel is therefore the form-text capable of narrating both, *d'Erec et d'Enide*: it is a marriage story, while the tale of the jesters is only of Erec ("d'Erec, le fil Lac, est li contes"), presenting itself plausibly as an adventure tale about the exploits of a young knight ('son of King Lac'). The authorial contrast between those who wrote of him and her – of husband and wife – and those who only tell about the knight is clearly a thematic contrast, a gap between two subjects – that of *avanture*, of Erec, and that of marriage, of Erec and Enide. The same dialectic actually recapitulates and reflects a structural opposition: that between *roman* and *conte*. Only the invention of the novel, that is, the *conjointure*, allows the plurality of narrative parts, characters and times – otherwise disjointed – to coexist and be contained in a single text, while the *conte d'avanture*, the ancient *modus narrandi*, is monodiegetic – able to develop only a single line of events, the exclusive one of chivalric adventure. Thus, that opposition in the incipit of *Cligès* gives us the clearest evidence of the 'conjugal plot' that determines the text-form, making the novel something quite different from the adventure tale.[17]

These poetic statements – placed at strategic points in the text – make it possible to interpret the *conjointure* as a technique able to transform a chivalric tale into an erotic-conjugal narrative. To reinforce this evidence, we can also consider the pragmatics of the text. It is in fact Chrétien himself who openly indicates the narrative point at which the *conjointure* is inserted. At line 1844, the narrator's voice intervenes in the work: "ci fine le premerains vers", 'here ends – literally – the first verse', the first part of the story, and thus what precedes this authorial statement constitutes a different narrative unit from what follows. Up until line 1844, the poet had in fact recapitulated the *conte d'avanture*, his so-called source, that is, that chivalric subject, widespread in courtly and jester tales, which he wanted to 'conjoin' to another story, to expand its narrative development into a novel. Before line 1844, the text had narrated the adventure of the white stag – the Arthurian court hunting the mythical animal – and the 'sub-adventure' of Erec, who, far from the hunters, is the guest of the castellan who will give him his daughter Enide in marriage. The vicissitudes of the white stag and the knight's personal ones – two hunts: of the animal and of the woman – are finally united with the return to court of the two future spouses, Erec and Enide, and with Arthur's kissing the girl. Having captured the stag, the king, by custom, can kiss the most beautiful woman in the court. It is therefore, up to verse 1844, a concluded and realised *entrelacement*:[18] two parallel adventures – that of the hunt and that of Erec towards his future wife – which end with the return to court of the knight and the girl, to whom the king's kiss is due.

The lexicon of the novel is also useful to emphasise how this 'first verse' corresponds thematically to the jesters' tale, that is, the adventure from which the poet, by way of opposition, wants to derive his novel (vv. 1841–1844):

Li rois por itel *avanture*
randi l'usage et la droiture
qu'a sa cort devoit li blans cers.
Ci fine le premerains vers.

[By this *adventure*, the king restored in his court the rule and custom of the white stag. Here ends the first verse]

Concluding the textual unit pertaining to the *conte d'avanture*, Chrétien makes explicit its accomplishment by recalling the key word *avanture* – "por itel avanture". It is the same adventure which, almost 2,000 lines earlier, as the incipit of the novel, differentiated two narrative forms: on the one hand the *conte d'avanture*, broken or shattered by jesters' narratives, and on the other the fictional *conjointure*. The latter would begin, then, from around line 1845 on, as the second and more authentic narrative plot. From this point on, the old jesters' tale is replaced by the authorial novel, centred on the marriage of Erec and Enide and their conjugal crisis – so profound as to split the couple into their respective ghosts (the episode of the *Joie de la cour*[19]) – and finally on the conclusive solution.

Recognising in the 'first verse' a virtually closed textual section,[20] an *entrelacement* fully realised, now requires further clarification. One often reads in critical exegeses that *conjointure* is simply a different name for the narrative technique of *entrelacement*: joining and tying together the different parts of the narrative so as to interweave them into the main story. This is a generalisation, perhaps excessive, by which the specific notion of *conjointure*, applied in the context of *Erec*, would represent the overall technique of the storyline – so as to assume the meaning of a general 'theory of the novel'. This perspective culminates in the hypothesis of a partial synonymy between *conjointure* and *entrelacement*.[21] However, the fact that Chrétien distinguishes the *entrelacement* of his 'first verse' – the *conte d'avanture* – from the rest of the novel, that is, from his personal *conjointure*, casts doubt on the equivalence of the two terms. It is certainly true that a *conjointure* produces new levels of storyline – and that the two operations therefore condition each other – but this does not imply that the two concepts have the same origin and function.

Indeed, the hypothesis I now formulate is that the *conjointure* has a precise, semantically narrower meaning, and that it derives from an identifiable source in classical poetics. Ultimately, I believe that the *mout bele conjointure* enunciated in the prologue to *Erec* should be read in the light of the *optima coniunctio*. This latter is the notion that Servius, the great late-antique commentator, developed to discuss the place of Book IV of the *Aeneid* in the context of the Virgil's poem as a whole. That is, the commentator had to justify this Book, narrating the obsessive love between Aeneas and Dido, being part of the Latin epic poem. By the notion of *optima coniunctio* Servius wished to demonstrate the poetic–narrative link between two distinct topics, apparently unrelated in terms of theme and literary genre: on the one hand the epic subject matter that constitutes the core of the *Aeneid*, and on the other the erotic-psychological drama narrated in Book IV. The issue was so

Conjointure 11

important that Servius sought the answer in the preliminary gloss to Virgil's Book IV.

> Hic liber [...] est autem paene totus in affectione, licet in fine pathos habeat, ubi abscessus Aeneae gignit dolorem. Sane totus in consiliis et subtilitatibus est; nam paene comicus stilus est; nec mirum, ubi de amore tractatur. *Iunctus* quoque superioribus est, quod artis esse videtur, ut frequenter diximus; nam ex abrupto vitiosus est transitus. Licet stulte quidam dicunt hunc tertio non esse *coniunctum* – in illo enim navigium, in hoc amores exsequitur – non videntes *optimam coniunctionem*; cum enim tertium sic clauserit 'factoque hic fine quievit', subsecutus 'at regina gravi iamdudum saucia cura', item paulo post 'nec placidam membris dat cura quietem'; nam cum Aenean dormire dixerit, satis congrue *subiunxit* ut somno amans careret.
>
> (Servius, *praefatio* to *Aeneid* IV)

[This book [...] is almost entirely about passion – yet it ends in pathos, when Aeneas's departure produces grief. In fact, the book is all full of dialogues and subtleties, and its style is almost comic – which is not surprising, since it is about love. Moreover, it is *conjoined* to the previous books, according to the rules of art, as has often been said – in fact, an abrupt transition is not correct. Yet some foolishly claim that this book is not *conjoined* to the third – in that one it speaks of sea voyages, in this one of love – but they do not understand the *perfect conjunction*. While the third book closes with the words 'factoque hic fine quievit', the other follows with 'at regina gravi iamdudum saucia cura', and shortly afterwards 'nec placidam membris dat cura quietem'. Since he had said that Aeneas slept, he *added accordingly* that his lover [Dido] did not sleep.]

It is necessary to fix all the points of the poetic argument, where Servius characterises the matter and style of the Virgilian Book IV. The glossator states that this Book deals with feelings (*affectione*), that is, human conditions, and then culminates in the pathetic close – with Aeneas's departure and Dido's suicide. The substance of the book is made up of speeches, words spoken or unspoken, tribulations and afterthoughts (*totus in consiliis et subtilitatibus*).[22] Its erotic feature, full of dialogue and disclosures, makes – says

12 Conjointure

Servius – the style of the Book 'almost comic' (*nam paene comicus stilus est*). According to an ancient or medieval grammarian, if the form is such as to be 'comic', the facts of the narration, the tragic events of a suicide for love, do not change the initial stylistic perception.[23] It should not be surprising – adds Servius – that the Book appears comic, given that it is about love. These love affairs, for the commentator, are in fact equivocal or vaguely intricate, like those in a comedy of Terence, who in fact will be the first *auctoritas* introduced as a gloss on the Book.[24] This diversity of subject matter and style poses the problems that the glossator immediately notes: those of the structural relationship between Book IV and the rest of the poem. What is the relationship between this erotic and 'almost comic' Book and the epic substance of the *Aeneid*? Unlike other readers, who evidently emphasised the fracture of the two parts (*quidam dicunt hunc tertio non esse coniunctum*), Servius defends the *optima coniunctio*. That is, he claims the 'perfect conjunction' between the epic Books, devoted to the voyage and arms (*navigium*), and the 'comic-erotic' Book of Aeneas and Dido (*amores*): 'he who says that Book IV is not conjoined to the third, does not understand the *optimam coniunctionem*'. Moreover, according to Servius, this 'perfect conjunction' is based on elements of narrative micro-syntax and verbal continuity. The commentator says: if the previous Book closes on Aeneas who, having finished speaking to Dido, falls silent and takes a rest (*factoque hic fine quievit*), Book IV opens on a contrasting conjuncture: the image of the queen who, victim of her desire for Aeneas, cannot sleep (*nec placidam membris dat cura quietem*). Aeneas's rest in contrast with Dido's sleeplessness, combined with the lexical repetition *quievit/quietem*, is sufficient, in Servius's formal perspective, to certify the excellent *coniunctio* of the two Books and the overall unity of the parts.

The exegetical material that Servius's gloss offers to the interpretation of Chrétien's novel seems structurally significant. By Servius's exegesis, we may be able to explain both the novel's overall *inventio* and its poetic device, namely the *mout bele conjointure*, which organises the plot. However, research on the semantics and origin of that expression has already yielded various results, which can be reduced in summary to three different readings of the concept. William A. Nitze's proposal[25] – later refined by first Douglas Kelly and then Claudia Villa[26] – derives the Old French *conjointure* from Horace's *Poetics* and in particular from its famous *callida iunctura* ('clever junction'). Horace understands the *iunctura* to be limited to the lexical and syntactical conjunction, that is, a brilliant link between words, but it has been shown that medieval tradition expanded its meanings. Medieval grammarians support, through Horace's idea, the possibility of a structural juncture of diegetic parts, that is, Horace's *iunctura* becomes a rule of narrative composition and not only a matter of syntax.

Recent hypotheses shift the referential sphere of Chrétien's *conjointure*. Lucia Lazzerini traces it back to a theological reading of the *Erec*, in which the *coniunctio* is derived from biblical exegesis and entails a semantics joining *littera* and *sensus*: the literal *fabula* (the *conte*) conjoined to its further meanings, as a result of allegory and anagoge in the text.[27] Finally, Dan Cepraga explains the genesis of *conjointure* within the framework of Aristotelian logic, in particular through the work of Boethius: in medieval analytics the *logoi* ('discourses') could be unitary through σύνδεσμος, that is, the *coniunctio* of the parts. For Aristotle, a classic example of this linguistic situation would be the *Iliad*, or rather diegetic-mimetic literature as a whole, whose signification is unitary by virtue of the conjunction of its narrative parts.[28]

A review of these interpretations, however they may differ from each other, nevertheless shows general agreement on some basic meanings: *conjointure* in Chrétien, whatever its sources, defines a writing process based on the articulation of two or more elements – whether rhetorical, symbolic–theological or logical–compositional.[29] The lemma in the respective source – *iunctura* or *coniunctio* – is to be found for each of these hypotheses, and, through its verbal transposition into Old French, applies its meaning to the fictional text. However, in my opinion, Servius's gloss allows for a different and less extrinsic analysis. Seen from his perspective, the Virgilian tradition[30] offers a sure morphological equivalent of the entire Old French syntagma: *coniunctio* and *conjointure*, *optima* and *mout bele*, forming an almost perfect translation. In addition, from a more internal and relevant perspective, Virgilian tradition can enlighten the entire matter of the novel, its *fabula* and structure. Our hypothesis is that Book IV of the *Aeneid* – with its erotic *argumentum* and its formal *coniunctio* – was deeply incorporated into Chrétien's novel; it is its actual thematic and stylistic palimpsest.

14 Conjointure

Indeed, the presence of Virgil's poem in Chrétien's work can thus be detected from several perspectives. Let us begin with the manuscript tradition.

More than half a century ago, there was a minor controversy over the extent of Chrétien's knowledge of Virgil. Jean Frappier intervened in the discussion around this issue[31] with a review of Werner Ziltener's 1957 book, *Chrétien und die Aeneis*, aiming to downplay any possible correspondence between Chrétien's work and the Virgilian model. However, I am suggesting we take up the 'Virgilian hypothesis' to explain the very meaning of the *conjointure* and to rehabilitate Chrétien's structuring relationship with Virgil as a whole.

Firstly, the tradition of the texts. The *Aeneid*, combined with different forms of Servius's glosses, is an absolutely documentable manuscript book in twelfth-century France. Chrétien could thus read one of those manuscripts that still attest the presence of Virgil and Servius in the ancient libraries of French clerics. By way of example, recall the Paris manuscript, BnF, lat. 7963, produced in the mid-twelfth century in northern France, or the well-known BnF, lat. 7930, also written in France, in the eleventh century. This latter manuscript sets out in categorical terms the contents of Servius' gloss: "iste liber totus comicus est" says the codex with regard to Book IV of the *Aeneid*. It later adds: "nam artis est finem precedentis libri initio sequentis *coniungere*", 'it is proper to art to *conjoin* the end of the preceding book with the beginning of the following one' (91r). That is, it establishes by means of two apophthegms the 'paradoxical' comic genre of Book IV and its compositional technique, that is, its *conjointure*.

Servius's gloss thus taught what a 'perfect conjuncture' was and how it should be constructed. According to its formalist approach, the *optima coniunctio* between two distinct narrative parts must be based on elements of verbal continuity and the repetition of certain elements of the subject matter, some 'episodic' features that preserve the flow of the *fabula*. Chrétien seems to respect both prerogatives quite literally.

Li rois por itel avanture
randi l'usage et la droiture
qu'a sa cort devoit li blans cers.
Ci fine le premerains vers.

- - - - *[conjointure]* - - - - - - - -
Quant li beisiers del cerf fu pris,
lonc la costume del païs,
Erec as cortois et frans
fu de son povre oste en espans
(vv. 1841–1848)

[By this adventure, the king restored the rule and custom of the white stag at his court. Here ends the first verse. // *conjointure* //. When the kiss of the stag was given, according to the custom of the country, Erec, as a noble and courteous man, took care of his poor host]

Lines 1845–1846 – "Quant li beisiers del cerf fu pris / lonc la costume del païs" – mark the beginning of the *conjointure*. Here, at the point where the first unit ends and the second narrative movement begins, Chrétien, as he had learnt from Servius, intentionally repeats facts and words from the previous section of the novel, according to a hyper-literalist practice with respect to Servius's gloss. In fact, the episode in which Arthur, after capturing the white stag, kisses Enide had just been referred to only a few lines earlier; it would thus be at the forefront of a reader's mind. If this episode is recalled again, it is because the words 'kiss' (*beisiers*), 'stag' (*cerf*), *droiture* and 'custom' are in Chrétien the textual marks of the *coniunctio*. They are the verbal and functional equivalents of the lemmas, 'quiet' and 'rest', repeated between Books III and IV of Virgil's poem and pointed out by Servius's gloss. Those words are, in short, the lexical connectives between the two parts of the novel.

After these lexical repetitions, there follows the 'episodic' connection through the recovery of previous narrative situations. In fact, once the *conjointure* has started, the first event narrated in this second part of the novel concerns an episode still pending from the first unit of the story. It concerns the dowry that Erec delivers to the parents of his future bride, Enide: they are feudal lords, as the novel states, noble but impoverished, and therefore in need of goods. Erec rewards them for giving him their daughter (vv. 1847–1854).

Erec as cortois et frans
fu de son povre oste en espans

16 Conjointure

> de ce que promis li avoit,
> covant mantir ne li voloit.
> Mout li tint bien son convenant,
> qu'il li anvoia maintenant
> cinc somiers sejornez et gras
> chargiez de robes et de dras
>
> [(When the kiss of the stag was given ...) Erec, as a noble and courteous man, took care of his poor host, about what he had promised him, for he did not want to break the pact. He fulfilled the agreement and immediately sent him five packhorses, well bred, laden with robes and drapery].

This episode immediately continues with an investiture: in addition to the gifts, Erec grants Enide's parents two castles from his lands. The narration of these details extends for some 60 lines, effectively constituting a thematic repetition, that is, a conjunction of subject matter with the previous narrative unit. It was in fact more than 500 lines earlier (vv. 1330–1333), still within the *conte d'avanture*, that Chrétien recounted how Erec had promised Enide's father the investiture and the castles if he obtained the girl's love.

> Mener vos ferai an la terre
> qui mon pere est et moie aprés;
> loing est de ci, n'est mie pres.
> Iluec vos donrai deus chastiaus
>
> [I will take you to the land that is now my father's and later will be mine – it is far from here; there I will give you two castles]

Strictly following the diegetic rules enunciated by the Servian *coniunctio* – which rejected the *transitus ex abrupto*, that is, the sudden passage to a new subject – Chrétien gradually opens his *conjointure*: he thus reconnects the story to a fact left unresolved by the previous narrative unit, the *conte*: the promise of a dowry to Enide's parents, which has yet to be fulfilled. Thanks to this diegesis, based on verbal and 'episodic' continuity, the *avanture* and the *conjointure* merge into each other. This narrative solution generates the novel as the only textual form capable of giving continuity to a subject matter that the old Muses, that is, the old jesters' tales, separated and fragmented into distinct spheres of subjects and styles. The resulting fictional text and the corresponding book thus finally assume modern forms.

Roland Barthes remarked:[32]

> The (traditional) Book is an object which *connects, develops, runs* and *flows*; in short, it has the deepest *horror vacui*. Sympathetic metaphors of the Book are: fabric to be woven, water flowing, [...], path to be followed [...]; antipathetic metaphors are those of a fabricated object, i.e. an object assembled out of discontinuous raw materials [...]. For what is hidden behind this condemnation of the discontinuity is obviously the myth of Life itself: the Book must *flow* [...]; to write is to secrete words within that great category of the *continuous* which is narrative.

Barthes's statement was polemical towards those critics who rejected analytical and fragmented writing, and the 'disorganised book', which Barthes himself defended. With the work of Chrétien, with the *conjointure* of *Erec* and the 'discovery of the novel' shortly after the mid-twelfth century, we are at the origins of the same problem conceived by the French critic eight centuries later. That is, we are at the point where the novel reveals itself as a textual form of continuity, as a unitary articulation of historical and existential variety.

Let us recall that, according to Servius's gloss, Virgil's Book IV – the palimpsest of the Old French novel – would have risked becoming a 'comedy', if it had been disjointed from the epic continuity with the rest of the poem. Let us also recall that for the *Tractatus coislinianus* and Greek poetics the secret of the comic genre was based on diegetic anacoluthon, that is, on the 'incongruity' and 'disconnection' of narrative outcomes. Therefore, preserving continuity, producing *conjointure* and simulating – as Barthes wrote – that life is a flux and that the novel replicates its flow and durations, ultimately means insisting on preserving the 'tragic' and 'heroic' aspects of representation. This search for continuity aims to avoid the narrative of an existence turning mimetically into a collection of scenes without an intrinsic link, that is, the 'comic' or buffoonish result par excellence.[33]

Chrétien de Troyes was certainly unaware of the entire classical and modern tradition that had focused on these poetic problems and would continue to do so. Nevertheless, he places the origin of his first novel precisely on that border: on the edge between tragedy and comedy, between unity and anacoluthon – conjunction and disconnection – and between the individual adventure – the 'comic' or jester's episode of an existential exploit – and the continuous and long-lasting destiny of a marriage story.[34] In this sense, it is highly probable that the Old French poet, on the one hand, derived his stylistic notion from the Virgilian *coniunctio* and, on the other, transposed the same notion on a level of semantic ambiguity. *Conjointure* would therefore be both the name of the narrative form and that of the narrated matter. That is, it would mean both the *optima coniunctio* of Servius's gloss and the *coniugium*, the marriage – with its crisis – of the two protagonists. They are the two sides of the same discovery: *littera* and form of the novel.

Let us now consider the thematic palimpsest. The latter emerges through those narrative sections that allow us to read in the novel's core the rewriting of Virgil's Book IV – thus doubling the meaning of the *conjointure*. In principle, Servius's gloss formulated a thematic bipartition that could be adapted to Chrétien's work. When the commentator distinguishes between the topics of Book III and Book IV – and then asks what connects them – he states that Book III deals with the *navigium*, that is, adventures and voyages, and Book IV with the *amores*, that is, the passion between Aeneas and Dido. In other words, Servius conceives the question of the *coniunctio* as a problem of the relation between the epic-heroic topic (*navigium*) and the erotic-psychological one (*amores*). The same 'heroic/erotic bipartition' operates in Chrétien's novel, namely in the relationship between the *conte d'avanture* – the vicissitudes of the white stag and Erec – and the marriage story that follows the *conjointure*.

It is, however, in the centre of the novel that we can detect the main Virgilian palimpsests: in the long sequence – turning points of the plot – in which Chrétien relates the crisis of the conjugal relationship between Erec and Enide. Having passed the *conjointure*, the two protagonists are now married. At first, the couple receive praise and admiration from the whole court and its barons, but quickly conjugal love degenerates into passion. Chrétien portrays the couple in amorous idleness, "boche a boche" (v. 2477, 'mouth to mouth'). He shows them in bed for a long time, until the afternoon, absorbed only in themselves, completely estranged from courtly society. This introverted bending of the conjugal relationship, almost a rejection or fear of the world, which is perceived as a threat to the lovers' seclusion, produces a hallucinatory and alternative cosmos for the couple. Erec fails in his chivalric duties; his companions-in-arms perceive the alteration, criticise and then mock him (vv. 2434–2468).

> Mes tant l'ama Erec d'amors
> que d'armes mes ne li chaloit,
> [...]
> a sa dame aloit dosnoiier.
> De li fist s'amie et sa drue.
> Tot mist son cuer et s'antendue
> an li acoler et beisier;
> ne se queroit d'el aeisier.
> Si compaignon duel an avoient;
> antr'aus sovant se demantoient
> de ce que trop l'amoit assez.
> Sovant estoit midis passez
> einçois que de lez li levast;
> lui estoit bel, qui qu'il pesast.
> Mout petit de li s'esloignoit
> [...].
> Tant fu balsmez de totes janz,
> de chevaliers et de serjanz,
> que Enide l'oï antredire
> que recreant aloit ses sire
> d'armes et de chevalerie;
> mout avoit changiee sa vie.

[Erec loved her so much that he neglected his weapons [...]; he lived only in the love of his wife and made her his mistress and beloved. All his desire and all his will were directed towards touching and kissing her, and only from her did he derive pleasure. His companions were troubled by this and often complained to one another about how excessively he loved her. Often it was past noon and he had not yet got up from beside her; but he liked it that way – even though the others complained about it; he hardly ever left his woman [...]. Then he was blamed by all, knights and servants alike, and so Enide heard murmurs that her husband was a layabout and renegade, relinquishing arms and chivalry, and that his life was much changed].

In this passage, we can identify the first traces of the Virgilian palimpsest, in particular of the Carthaginian episode or of the *Didotema* ('the topic of Dido') – as Ziltener has aptly defined it.[35] The palimpsest of the classical poem extends from here for at least the next 300 lines, that is, until the point at which Erec decides to return to his life as a knight, setting off on adventures, accompanied by his wife. In this regard, Frappier's objections do not seem convincing: he denied the relationship between Chrétien and Virgil, since by his analysis he did not find any exact identification of the French characters with corresponding figures in the Latin poem. Actually, the contact between the two works is much deeper than a mere correspondence between characters: Book IV of the *Aeneid* delivered to the novel of *Erec* an overall representation centred on a shared literary topic: the *recreantise* ('unwillingness', or 'disowning himself'). This Old French lemma describes a psychological situation of self-rejection such that one forgets who one is, to the point of denying one's destiny: this is actually both the *Didotema* in the Virgilian poem and the *recreantise* in the novel. Enide therefore overhears the barons and knights accusing Erec of being *recreant*, that is, a renegade who neglects weapons and lives in an idle turmoil of his passions: "Enide l'oï antredire / que *recreant* aloit ses sire / d'armes et de chevalerie".

A comparison of passages from the *Aeneid* and the novel of *Erec* will show how the topic of idle unwillingness deeply affects both works. In the Latin poem, moreover, the theme does not only concern Aeneas, who is held back in Carthage by his and Dido's passion, while the gods order him to take *Latium* – "regnum Italiae Romanaque tellus" (IV, 275). The same reluctance actually afflicts the queen as well. The lonely passion that binds Dido and the Trojan – in a cave and in the palace – on the one hand distracts Aeneas from the fate of Rome, and on the other forces the Carthaginian queen to renounce all care for her kingdom. For this reason, Virgil calls both "regnorum immemores" (IV, 194), 'oblivious of kingdoms' and all duty. Moreover, from the very beginning of the Book he had described the effects of love on the city of Carthage, now forgotten by the queen (IV, 86–88).

Non coeptae adsurgunt turres, non arma iuventus
exercet portusve aut propugnacula bello
tuta parant: pendent opera interrupta.

[The towers that have been started do not grow, the youth are not trained with weapons, and no safe harbour or bastions are built: the works remain unfinished.]

This is Dido's *recreantise*: a queen whose obsessive love has made her a recluse who neglects government. Her oblivion is equivalent to that of Aeneas, whose idleness in the Latin poem was reproached by the gods: "nulla accendit tantarum gloria rerum / nec super ipse sua molitur laude laborem", 'no glory of great things entices him nor does he want to toil for his fame'. Shared by both classical lovers, we find the same guilt, the same *recreantise* as Erec's. Chrétien's hero, in fact, has «relanquie / [...] tote chevalerie» (vv. 2503–2504): because of love, he has forsaken all endeavour and remained without weapons – "armes antreleissiez" (v. 2547). It is the same rejection expressed by Aeneas, who renounced *tantarum gloria rerum* and whose signs of heroism – his weapons – hung idly on his lover's bed – "arma viri / thalamo quae fixa reliquit" (IV, 495). It is also the same situation as Dido's Carthage, where young men no longer practise chivalry. Finally, it must be noted that in both the Latin poem and the Old French novel this rejection of one's destiny is a *relinquere* (*relanquie / reliquit*), that is, another name for *recreantise*.

In short, here are the tragic effects of the introverted, obsessive passion that binds the two Latin characters: a city that falls apart and a hero with no more feats to perform. *Recreant*, that is, idle and reluctant: in the classical poem it is the couple as a whole, and not the man alone who are described thus. That is why, in the comparison with the Old French novel, those exact mirror images that Frappier demanded are not possible. The relationship does not lie in the equation Enide = Dido on the one hand, Erec = Aeneas on the other. On the contrary, Chrétien's two characters can share, or exchange, both Dido's and Aeneas's features at the same time. Indeed, it is sometimes Erec, the man, who most clearly expresses the poetic memory of the Carthaginian queen, while in the woman, though this is little appreciated by critics,[36] her name, Enide, echoes Aeneas and the *Aeneid*.

The *mout bele conjointure* – derived from Servius's *optima coniunctio* – was thus for Chrétien the conjunction in the same work of the heroic issue with the erotic one. In this sense, the whole of Virgil's Book IV, that is, the textual place of the *coniunctio* in the classical poem, is transferred to the novelistic core of *Erec*. *Recreantise* is not only – somewhat too simply – the conflict between duty and passion, but is rather, and from a narrative perspective, the very possibility of the novel as a heroic-erotic genre,[37] as an intertwined space between tragedy and comedy.

Many centuries later, we recover in Balzac the meaning of Chrétien's verses on the erotic degeneration of the couple: "de li fist s' amie et sa drue" – we read in the Old French novel – Erec turned his wife to 'a mistress'. In *Cousine Bette*, about the fictional couple Hortense-Venceslaus, Balzac writes: "une immense preuve d'infériorité chez un homme que de ne pas savoir faire de sa femme sa maîtresse", 'it is an enormous proof of inferiority in a man not to know how to turn his wife into his mistress'. The novelistic issue, namely its heroic-erotic topic, from Virgil's Book IV to Balzac's *Cousine*, via Chrétien, is centred around this cleavage. The pathological psychic regression that affects Erec and Enide, a married couple, and reduces them to a pair of lovers, isolated and almost clandestine, must be compared with Dido's reverse but identical hallucination. The queen mistakes her passionate fury for a marriage union – "nec iam furtivum Dido meditatur amorem; / coniugium vocat, hoc praetexit nomine culpam" (IV, 171–172), 'Dido does not imagine a furtive love; she calls it a union, and with this name she covers her guilt'.

In the Old French novel, therefore, the main scene in which Chrétien represents the conjugal problem – that is, the acknowledgement of the couple's isolation – seems to expand the effects of the *coniunctio* theorised by Servius. For the late antique commentator, the link between Book III and Book IV was largely based on the continuous image of sleep: Aeneas resting, Dido unable to sleep because of her anxious passion. The topic of sleep runs through Virgil's entire book and, in fact, we find it repeated later, when by now Aeneas is plotting his escape and the queen's madness increases (IV, 530–555). Virgil calls Dido "infelix Phoenissa neque umquam solvitur somnos", 'the sorrowful Phoenician who never takes sleep'. At the same time, he reiterates the contrast with Aeneas's sleep: "Enea celsa in puppi, iam certus eundi, / carpebat somnos", 'Aeneas, on the high stern, now confident of leaving, took sleep'.

The opposition sleep/wake, which characterises Book IV and which Servius identified as the main device of *optima coniunctio*, structures in Chrétien the entire central scene of the novel and thus reaffirms the origin of the *conjointure*. It is the scene in which Enide, still in the secrecy of the bedroom, confesses to her husband that the court accuses him of *recreantise*, because of their union. As in Virgil, the woman cannot sleep, while the man seems immersed in a sleep of unconsciousness (vv. 2479–2482).

Cil dormi, et cele veilla.
De la parole li manbra,
que disoient de son seignor
par la contree li pluisor

[He slept and she kept vigil. Enide remembered the word that all over the country many people were repeating about her husband].

When Enide confesses, in a diegetic perspective, the actual narrative problem – namely the *recreantise* – Erec sleeps like Virgil's Aeneas, while she replicates Dido's sleeplessness. A further palimpsest also emerges in those verses: the *pluisor*, the 'multitude' that murmurs and blames the couple (vv. 2544–2565).

Par ceste terre dïent tuit,
li noir et li blont et li ros,
que granz domages est de vos
que vos armes antreleissiez.
[...]
Recreant vos apelent tuit.
[...]
Blasmee en sui, ce poise moi,
et dïent tuit que reison por quoi,
que si vos ai lacé et pris
que tot an perdez vostre pris,
ne querez a el antendre

[In this land, everyone – black, blonde or red – says it is very bad for you to give up weapons [...]. Everyone calls you idle and renegade [...]. They accuse me of this, everyone says that the cause is that I dominate you to the point that you lose your valour and devote yourself to nothing else.]

The *pluisor*, or *tuit*, are a collective character, a malicious and impersonal voice, whose murmuring in the novel offends and reveals the couple's error. In the *Aeneid*, this identical function had already been represented by the prosopopoeia of Fame. The goddess, flying over Carthage, spread the news of how Aeneas and Dido lived. "Haec tum multiplici populos sermone replebat / [...] / nunc hiemen inter se luxu, quam longa, fovere / regonrum immemores turpique cupidine captos" (IV, 189–194), Fame 'filled the people with many speeches [...], said that they now spent the winter alone in lust, oblivious of the kingdoms, consumed by a repugnant passion'. Chrétien's insistence that everyone – *chevalier* and *serjanz*, nobles, servants and *pluisor* – blamed the couple, could also be explained as an amplification of Servius's gloss. With regard to lines 186–187 of Book IV about Fame, Servius had described the multitude of murmurers: "per domos nobilium [...], per regum domos [...], magnos populos; et dicit plebeios", 'nobles, kings and commoners'.

However, in neither Virgil nor Chrétien is the emphasis placed on the immorality of the relationship between the male and female characters: the problem is not the sensuality that binds the lovers, but the deeper relationship between the heroic and the erotic life, the possibility of the two lives coexisting. Only in this sense can the problem also concern a married, non-adulterous couple like that of Erec and Enide. Moreover, Virgil himself tells of the god Mercury who, in order to lead Aeneas from *recreantise* back to his destiny, accuses him of being Dido's ridiculous husband: "Tu nunc Karhaginis altae / fundamenta locas pulchramque uxorius urbem / exstruis" (IV, 265–267), 'now you build the high foundations of Carthage and like a husband you raise a beautiful city'. Servius glossed these lines with the biting definition "uxori serviens", 'the wife's servant'.

The fact that even the conjugal state – the life of husband and wife – can hinder the heroic life reveals, incidentally, the Christian root of the narrative problem in the Old French poet. Indeed, in the Middle Ages the supreme model of heroic life is the clerical life: it is holiness, of which chivalry in the twelfth century becomes a reflection. From St. Paul to St. Jerome, passing through monastic theology, the Christian tradition suspects that marriage entails the 'narrative end' of the hero-saint. The protagonist of a hagiographic tale of St. Jerome makes the problem explicit in the following words: "Vale, [...], infelix mulier; habeto me martyrem potius quam maritum", 'farewell, my unlucky wife, keep me as a martyr rather than as a husband'.[38] The same theme continues directly in the Romance literatures: for instance, in *Saint Alexis*, the first Romance hero, and his escape from his wife – "se or ne m'en fui [...]" (v. 60).[39]

In Chrétien's narrative invention we can observe further overlaps and exchanges between his characters and the Virgilian model. In the classical poem it is the male hero, Aeneas, who becomes conscious of *recreantise* – conditioned by the accusations of the gods (vv. 265–294) – while in the Old French novel it is the woman, Enide – influenced by the murmurings of the knights – who becomes aware of their guilt, of that isolation more befitting two lovers than two spouses. Chrétien prefigures in this opposite mirroring, between the Virgilian male hero and his female character, the equivalence that will later become explicit towards the novel's conclusion. This final equivalence will develop into a fundamental paronomasia: *Aeneid* = Enide. Aeneas, the Trojan character of the Latin poem, and Enide, the wife of the Old French novel, become equally aware that their erotic behaviour precludes the heroic life. Both immediately experience the problem of communicating to the other – to Dido or to Erec – the content of this new awareness. In both the poem and the novel, the 'Aeneids', that is, Aeneas and Enide, fear the consequences of the word they will have to utter.

> Heu quod agit? Quo nunc reginam ambire furentem
> audeat adfatu? Quae prima exordia sumat?
> Atque animun nunc huc celerem, nunc dividit illuc
>
> (IV, 283–285)

[Alas, what to do? With what words will [Aeneas] dare to circumvent the delirious queen? Whence shall he begin to speak? He divides his quick mind here and there.]

Having overcome these hesitations, Aeneas resolves to prepare to escape, before he has even uttered the 'word', before he has even informed Dido that his *recreantise* has ended. Thus, the queen's desperate invective against the reticent Aeneas is based precisely on this: on the accusation that he wanted to leave her in silence, in secret, without saying a word (IV, 305–306).

> Dissimulare etiam sperasti, perfide, tantum
> Posse nefas *tacitusque* mea decedere terra?

[Oh perfidious one, did you hope to feign such cruelty and leave, *without a word*, my land?]

Servius explains the lemma of these lines as follows: "Dissimulare [...], ac si diceret 'ita rem pudendam cogitas ut eam fateri nolis'", 'dissimulate, like saying: "you think something so shameful that you don't dare speak"'. Servius had previously commented on Aeneas's hesitations – whether to say or not to say, and how to say, to Dido that he planned to escape from their *recreantise*: "et per hoc ostenditur cogitasse eum etiam amorem sed praetulisse voluntatem deorum", 'in this way it is shown that Aeneas inclined to love, but obeyed the order of the gods'.

The condition of Aeneas, narrated by Virgil and glossed by Servius, is thus the exact condition of Enide. It is the problem of the 'word' to be spoken, of the new awareness to be communicated to her lover. In both characters, the hesitation between silence and 'word' corresponds to the hesitation between prolonging the amorous pleasures and, in contrast, a confession that, while saving the hero's fate, would destroy the symbiosis of passion.

> Cil dormi, et cele veilla.
> De la parole li manbra,
> que disoient de son seignor
> par la contree li pluisor.
> [...]
> Tel duel en ot et tel pesance
> qu'il li avint par mescheance
> que ele dist une parole
> don ele se tint puis por fole
> [...]
> Et dist: 'Lasse, con mar m' esmui
> de mon païs! Que ving ça querre?
> Bien me devroit sorbir la terre,
> quant toz li miaudre chevaliers
> [...]

a del tot an tot relanquie
por ma tote chevalerie'
(vv. 2479–2504)

[He was asleep and she was awake. Enide remembered the word that many people all over the country were repeating about her husband. […] She felt such pain and burden that she finally let something slip away – and for this reason, she later thought herself mad. […] She said: 'Alas, for what misfortune have I left my country? What have I come to seek here? I deserve to be swallowed up by the earth,[40] since the best knight has given up all chivalric endeavour for me'].

In any case, Enide finally speaks. Erec, who is asleep, hears her voice and at once makes her explain the reason for her lament. Having become aware of the accusation of *recreantise*, Erec decides to leave and resume his life of chivalry. From this moment on, the wife vents her regret: at first, she denies having said anything, then, having to admit *la parole* ('the word'), she is ashamed of having uttered it (vv. 2509–2608).

Erec ne dormi pas formant,
si l'a tresoï an dormant.
de la parole s'evella
[…]
'Sire, fet ele, je ne sai
neant de quan que vos me dites
[…]
Quel forsenage osai dire?
Deus! Don ne m'amoit trop mes sire?
An foi, lasse, trop m'amoit il
[…]
Li miaudre hon, qui onques fust nez,
S'estoit si vers moi atornez
que d'autre rien ne li chaloit;
nule chose ne me faloit;
Mout estoie de bonne eüree
mes trop m'a orguiauz sorlevee:
an mon orguel avrai domage,
quant ja ai dit si grant outrage'.

[Erec was not sleeping soundly, he heard her and because of that word he woke up [...]. 'Sir', she said, 'I don't know what you are talking about [...] What madness have I dared to utter? My God, did not my husband love me too much? Truly, yes, he loved me too much [...]. The best knight who ever lived was so ardent for me that he cared for nothing else; and I lacked nothing. I was so happy that I was driven to pride: and for my pride I shall be punished, for voicing such an outrage'.]

Enide thus contradicts herself: on the one hand, she becomes aware of the *recreantise* and, on the other, regrets confessing it to her husband and thereby undoing the couple's solitude. The wife in Chrétien's novel thus performs the functions of the classical Aeneas, bringing about the unexpected awakening from amorous idleness. From the Virgilian hero she also derives lexical elements: "et dist: 'Lasse, con mar m'esmui / de mon païs! Que ving ça querre?'", '"she says: alas, for what misfortune have I left my country? What have I come to seek here?"'. This sudden dismissal of the country in which the couple's obsessive relationship had taken place is comparable to Aeneas's similar rejection of Dido's lands: "ardet abire fuga dulcisque relinquere terras" (IV, 281), 'he desires to escape and leave the sweet lands'. At the same time, by virtue of the profound *conjointure*, Enide also plays the role of Dido, of the woman who cannot resist the end of the relationship. In this way, the textual mirroring multiplies: Enide, like Dido, would not want to renounce amorous solitude and yet, like Aeneas, she regrets having spoken and would have preferred instead to remain silent – *tacitus* (IV, 306), like Aeneas in front of the queen.

The echoes, both direct and inverse, between the Latin poem and the Old French novel are often pervasive. In Erec, as in the Virgilian Aeneas, we can detect a semantics linked to the topic of the 'long wait' engendered by *recreantise*, which is followed by the sudden desire to interrupt amorous idleness:

indulges hospitio causasque innecte *morandi* (IV, 51)
[extend hospitality and invent reasons to *remain*]

qua spe inimica gente *moratur* (IV, 235),
[with which hope does he *remain* among the enemies]

que trop me fet *demorer* ici (*Erec et Enide*, v. 2668),
[it makes me *remain* too long]

With regard to Enide, her textual dialectic with Dido appears in other details. The Carthaginian queen for a moment imagines herself following Aeneas and leaving with him: "iliacas igitur classes atque ultima Teucrum / iussa sequar? [...] / Quid tum? Sola fuga nautas comitabor ovantis?" (IV, 537–543) 'Will I follow the Trojan ships as their last slave? And then? Will I follow the jubilant sailors alone in their escape?' For Dido the idea of following her lover is just one more moment of madness. Following her husband, on the other hand, will be Enide's destiny: the wife will indeed accompany Erec in his endeavours, but be forced to remain silent – and thereby she expiates the guilt of her *parole*.

At this point of the analysis, the Virgilian palimpsest is reversed into a properly medieval ideological perspective: in fact, unlike the adulterous couple of the Latin poem, the conjugal couple of Chrétien, freed from the *recreantise* and idleness of lovers, can continue their exploits together. This concept will be expressed – almost as in a proverb – in a later couplet. When Erec has now passed the final adventure – the 'Joy of the court' – freeing two unmarried lovers from their loneliness, the woman of this second idle couple will ask Enide through what adventure she had obtained Erec's love. Enide clarifies in one line the ideological difference between herself and the other woman – who, moreover, is her cousin: "'or me redites / [...] / de vostre ami la verité, / par quel avanture il vos a'. / 'Bele cousine, il m'esposa'" (vv. 6290–6294), 'now tell me the truth about your friend: by what adventure he conquered you'. / 'My dear cousin, he married me'. Once again, the lemma *avanture* returns in the novel – "par quel avanture il vos a" – and once again, this lemma is presented as a dialectical and alternative pole to the semantics of *conjointure*. Enide in fact did not obtain Erec's love *par avanture*, but rather through a nuptial *conjointure* – "il m'esposa", 'he married me'.

In Chrétien's marriage plot, there is ultimately a continuous crossover with Virgil's lovers: Erec and Enide display from time to time features and prerogatives of both Aeneas and Dido. This is because the Old French poet did not simply transfer a 'classical source' into his *conjointure*, but rather an overall narrative topic. Thus, the subject of the novel is not the adventure of a knight, that is, the individual circumstances of the hero – of a new Aeneas – but rather the *conjointure* of a couple. These symmetries clearly appear in lines 5337–5346. Close to the novel's epilogue, Enide receives a horse with all its equipment as a gift. The description of this latter has sometimes been read in a purely ecphrastic key. Actually, in light of the Virgilian palimpsest, this description is the climax of the rewriting performed by Chrétien on the text of the *Aeneid*.

> Li arçon estoient d'ivoire,
> S'i fu antailliee l'estoire
> comant Eneas vint de Troie,
> comant a Cartage a grant joie
> Dido en son lit le reçut,
> comant Eneas la deçut,
> comant ele por lui s'ocist,
> coment Eneas pui conquist
> Laurente et tote Lombardie
> don il fu rois tote sa vie

[The horse's saddle was made of ivory and carved with the story of how Aeneas came from Troy, how in Carthage Dido joyfully received him in her bed, how Aeneas deceived her and she killed herself, and how Aeneas then conquered Latium and Lombardy, of which he was king for life.]

Enide's saddle, decorated with the bas-relief of the *Aeneid*, constitutes the novel's analepsis, its *mise en abyme* and its definitive recapitulation. In those lines, moreover – in addition to the almost exhaustive compendium of the Latin poem – we can identify some Virgilian textual references. In the novel, "comant Eneas vint de Troie" seems to echo Virgil's line from Book IV, "venisse Aenean Troiano" (IV, 191); the lines about 'the bed in which Aeneas was received' and for which Dido then killed herself also evoke the Latin text: "Dido en son lit le reçut / [...] / comant ele por lui s'ocist", to be compared with the 'lectum iugalem / quo perii' (IV, 496–497), 'the conjugal bed for which I died', in the words of Virgil's Dido herself.

Finally, beyond these textual correspondences, it is crucial to understand how, in the Old French novel, the sculpted saddle is solely and expressly addressed to Enide. She shows – by her very name – the clearest signs of the identification, and not with a single classical character but with the entire Virgilian story. Enide personifies the whole of the Latin poem, recapitulates it in her own character. Enide, in this sense, on top of her horse, materially transforms herself into the book of the *Aeneid*. She is the book, Enide is the *Aeneid*; a woman-book, in which two male narcissisms are realised. The 'narcissism of Erec', of the character-husband, who mirrors himself in the 'wife's book' in order to read and realise himself, and the 'narcissism of the poet', of Chrétien, who turns the woman into a sheet of parchment, on which to rewrite his ancient model – the Virgilian poem. The paronomasia between Enide and *Aeneid* foreshadowed this outcome from the very beginning. From a specifically onomastic point of view, it is then at least interesting to observe that Erec and Enide – names otherwise unknown in courtly narrative – are an anagram of *Creedieen*, almost homophonic with the poet's name. Ultimately, one might suspect that Chrétien, in rewriting his Latin model, disguised himself and the Virgilian book in the name of the two spouses.

Notes

1 That is, a compendium inspired by Aristotle's *Poetics*, transmitted by a tenth-century Byzantine codex (Paris, BnF, Coislin 120). As a pure hypothesis, some critics suggest that the *Tractatus* may preserve extracts from the lost Aristotelian book on comedy – see Janko 1984.
2 Foerster 1890, 1–2.
3 See Cepraga 2007.
4 See D'Agostino 2013 and Paradisi 2002. A contrastive analysis of the 'narratives of ancient matter' and Chrétien's novel was already proposed by Nitze (1914).
5 Other hypotheses range from the 1160s to the 1180s.
6 See Roncaglia 1981. Concerning Chrétien's work and the name of his narrative technique (between *roman* and *conjointure*), see Nitze 1915.
7 Genette 1972, 75.
8 Eco 1979, 38.
9 Ibid., 45.
10 Ibid., 49.
11 Genette 1972, 75.
12 See Maddox 1978 – as well as Uitti's 1981 review and Collins 1984. With regard to the marriage plot, see the 'legal analysis' of Colonna 2002.
13 The marriage problem, as a narrative problem, is attested in much Christian and medieval literature. Between the fourth and sixth centuries, the earliest hagiographies often identified the drama of the

hero-saint – his diegetic and dramaturgic function – precisely in the 'marriage risk'. By marrying, the protagonist of the 'hagiographic novels' undermines his heroic and narrative status – see Mainini 2020.
14 This is the hypothesis of Lazzerini (2000).
15 See Uitti 1981 and Barbiellini Amidei 2014.
16 Foerster 1888, 1. Concerning Virgilian echoes in the incipit of *Cligès*, see Beckmann 2004. He compares the Old French verse – *cil qui fist* ... – with "Ille ego qui ...", that is, to the alternative incipit of the *Aeneid*, well known to the medieval readers of Servius (Rand 1946).
17 Even the readings that evaluate the conjugal question risk underestimate its relevance. For example, regarding the 'marriage crisis' between the two protagonists – the core of the story – some readers speak of a 'merely transitional' narrative structure (Ryding 1971, 126).
18 About notion of *entrelacement*, see Chase 1983.
19 See Meneghetti 1976.
20 Frappier (1957, 89) described this section as "petit roman idyllique".
21 See Berthelot 1993, 51: the *conjointure* "constitutes in some way the initial basis for the *entrelacement*".
22 Just think of Dido's conversations with her sister Anna: "Anna, fatebor enim, miseri post fata Sychaei / coniugis [...], / solus hic inflexit sensus [...]" (IV, 20–22), 'Anna, I admit it, after the death of Sicheus, my unlucky husband, only Aeneas has troubled my senses ...'.
23 See Anderson 1981.
24 Servius quotes the comedy *Eunuchus*: "Iamdudum aut nimium, ut Terentius: 'iamdudum te amat; iamdudum illi facile sit quod doleat'".
25 Nitze 1915.
26 Kelly 1970; Villa 1996.
27 Lazzerini 2000.
28 Cepraga 2007.
29 See Azzam, Collet, Foehr-Janssens 2007.
30 See Mora-Lebrun 1994.
31 Frappier 1959. In addition, see Schulze-Busacker 2004.
32 Barthes 1972, 84; italics in original.
33 On the 'comic event' as a 'contingent and disjointed happening', see Köhler 1990, 31.
34 In the past, the perception of this narrative form was not fully understood by critics, who judged Chrétien's novel as a disconnected work: "*Erec* est un roman fort décousu, comprenant au moins trois parties qui n'ont entre elles aucun lien intime [...]. La première est un petit roman fort agréable, quoique déparé par quelques-unes des absurdités ordinaires des romans bretons [...]. Cette introduction ne tient en rien à la suite, non plus que l'épisode de la 'joie de la cour' [...] ne tient à ce qui le précède". Paris 1891, 158–159.

35 Ziltener 1957, 64–66; see Wittig 1970.
36 "Enide (dont le nom évoque Enéas et le monde virgilien)", Poiron 1986, 141.
37 See Segre 1984, 74.
38 *Vita Malchi monachi captivi*, V, 20. The Latin text contains a play on words between *martyrem* and *maritum*.
39 Perugi 2000, 169.
40 See Chrétien's verse *Bien me devroit sorbir la terre* and the analogous Virgilian verse *Sed mihi vel tellus optem prius ima dehiscat* (IV, 24).

References

W.S. Anderson, "Servius and the 'Comic Style' of Aeneid 4", *Arethusa*, 14 (1981), pp. 115–125.

W. Azzam, O. Collet, Y. Foehr-Janssens, "Cohérence et éclatement: réflexion sur les recueils littéraires du Moyen Âge", *Babel*, 16 (2007), pp. 31–59.

B. Barbiellini Amidei, "Joie de la cort / joie de l'acort. L'armonia degli elementi discordi nell'*Erec et Enide*", *Carte romanze*, 2 (2014), pp. 217–236.

R. Barthes, "Literature and Discontinuity", *Salmagundi*, 18 (1972), pp. 82–93 [or. ed. in *Critique*, 1962].

G.A. Beckmann, "Les premiers vers du Cligès", *Romania*, 122 (2004), pp. 202–205.

A. Berthelot, "The Romance as Conjointure of Brief Narratives", *L'Esprit créateur*, 33 (1993), pp. 51–60.

D.O. Cepraga, "*Conjointure:* ipotesi su un termine feticcio del romanzo", in *Parole e temi del romanzo medievale*, ed. A.P. Fuksas, Roma, Viella, 2007, pp. 67–82.

C.J. Chase, "Sur la théorie de l'entrelacement. Ordre et désordre dans le *Lancelot en prose*", *Modern Philology*, 80 (1983), pp. 227–241.

F. Collins, "A semiotic approach to Chrétien de Troyes *Erec et Enide*", *Interpretations*, 15 (1984), pp. 285–298.

D. Colonna, "Diritto e matrimonio nei romanzi cortesi di Chrétien de Troyes", *Materiali per una storia della cultura giuridica*, 52 (2022), pp. 3–24.

D.A. D'Agostino, *Il Medioevo degli antichi. I romanzi francesi della "Triade classica"*, Milano, Mimesis, 2013.

U. Eco, *Lector in fabula. La cooperazione interpretativa nei testi narrativi*, Milano, Bompiani, 1979.

W. Foerster (ed.), *Cligés von Christian von Troyes*, Halle, Max Niemeyer, 1888.

W. Foerster (ed.), *Erec und Enide von Christian von Troyes*, Halle, Niemeyer, 1890.

J. Frappier, *Chrétien de Troyes. L'homme et l'œuvre*, Paris, Hatier-Boivin, 1957.
J. Frappier, "Virgile source de Chrétien de Troyes?" *Romance Philology*, 13 (1959), pp. 50–58.
G. Genette, *Figures III*, Paris, Seuil, 1972.
R. Janko, *Aristotle on Comedy. Towards a reconstruction of Poetics II*, Berkeley and Los Angeles, University of California Press, 1984.
D. Kelly, "The Source and Meaning of Conjointure in Chrétien's *Erec*", *Viator* 1 (1970), pp. 179–200.
E. Köhler, *Il romanzo e il caso. Da Stendhal a Camus*, Bologna, Il Mulino, 1990 [or. ed. E. Köhler, *Der literarische Zufall. Das Mögliche und die Notwendigkeit*, München, Wilhelm Fink, 1973].
L. Lazzerini, "Gli enigmi di Chrétien de Troyes: un 'senso ulteriore' in *Erec et Enide*?" in *Carmina semper et citharae cordi. Études de philologie et métrique offerts à Aldo Menichetti*, Genève, Slatkine, 2000, pp. 117–134.
D. Maddox, *Structure and Sacring. The Systematic Kingdom in Chrétien's Erec et Enide*, Lexington, French Forum, 1978.
L. Mainini, "'Clerc' e 'chevalier'. L'identità dell'*Erec*", in *Confini e parole. Identità e alterità nell'epica e nel romanzo*. Atti del Convegno (21–22 settembre 2017), ed. A. Perrotta, L. Mainini, Roma, Sapienza Università Editrice, 2020, pp. 91–106.
M.L. Meneghetti, "'Joie de la cort': intégration individuelle et métaphore sociale dans *Erec et Enide*", *Cahiers de civilisation médiévale*, 19 (1976), pp. 371–379.
F. Mora-Lebrun, *L'Enéide médiévale et la naissance du roman*, Paris, Presses Universitaires de France, 1994.
W.A. Nitze, *The Romance of Erec, Son of Lac*, *Modern Philology*, 11 (1914), pp. 445–489.
W.A. Nitze, "*Sans* et *matière* dans les œuvres de Chrétien de Troyes", *Romania*, 44 (1915), pp. 14–36.
G. Paradisi, *Le passioni della storia. Scrittura e memoria nell'opera di Wace*, Roma, Bagatto, 2002.
G. Paris, Review of *Erec und Enide, von Christian von Troyes*, ed. W. Foerster, Halle, Niemeyer, 1870, *Romania*, 20 (1891), pp. 148–166.
M. Perugi (ed.), *La vie de Saint Alexis*, Genève, Droz, 2000.
D. Poiron, *Résurgences. Mythe et littérature à l'âge du symbole (XIIe siècle)*, Paris, Presses Universitaires de France, 1986.
E.K. Rand, J.J. Savage, H.T. Smith, G.B. Waldrop, J.P. Elder, B.M. Peebles, A.F. Stocker (eds.), *Servianorum in Vergilii Carmina Commentariorum quod in Aeneidos libros I et II explanationes continet*, vol. II, Lancaster, Pennsylvania, 1946.
A. Roncaglia, *Tristano e Anti-Tristano. Dialettica di temi e d'ideologie nella narrativa medievale*, Roma, Bulzoni, 1981, pp. 92–115.

W.W. Ryding, *Structure in Medieval Narrative*, The Hague and Paris, De Gruyter, 1971.
E. Schulze-Busacker, "La culture littéraire de Chrétien de Troyes", *Romania*, 122 (2004), pp. 289–319.
C. Segre, 'Quello che Bachtin non ha detto. Le origini medievali del romanzo', in Id., *Teatro e romanzo*, Torino, Einaudi, 1984, pp. 61–84.
K. Uitti, Review of D. Maddox, *Structure and Sacring. The Systematic Kingdom in Chrétien's* Erec et Enide, *French Forum*, 5 (1980), pp. 56–61.
K. Uitti, "À propos de philologie", *Littérature*, 41 (1981), pp. 30–46.
C. Villa, "Per 'Erec', 14: 'une molt bele conjointure'", in *Studi di filologia medievale offerti a D'Arco Silvio Avalle*, Milano and Napoli, Ricciardi, 1996, pp. 453–472.
J.S. Wittig, "The Aeneas-Dido Allusion in Chrétien's *Erec et Enide*", *Comparative Literature*, 22 (1970), pp. 237–253.
W. Ziltener, *Chrétien und die* Aeneis. *Eine Untersuchung des Einflusses von Vergil auf Chrétien de Troyes*, Graz and Köln, Hermann Böhlaus, 1957.

2 Books of stories and books of novels

1 The reader-character, the book-character

As we have just seen, the 'book of Enide' seems to be a mirror image of the 'book of Chrétien'. The Virgilian codex, read by the Old French poet, reappears along the text in the form of the female character.

In the history of the novel genre – from its origins to the literary canon of the nineteenth and twentieth centuries – we can often observe a complex relationship between the narrative text and the book that contains it. In other words, in the founding moments for the history of the novel, it is easy to discern a systematic relationship between the narrative text, placed in the present of its writing, and, conversely, the image of a book that has already been written. This latter, as literary topos, performs the functions of a pre-existing or imaginary book in which a new narrative – yet to be written – will be reflected. According to the hypothesis we have formulated in Chapter 1, the *Erec* novel hides and reflects the Virgilian book. Moreover, a number of 'hidden books' also reappear elsewhere in Chrétien's works. Their functions sometimes match more simple and typified narrative needs, such as the authorial need to gain credibility through the memory of a 'rediscovered book'. This happens, for instance, in *Cligés*, where Chrétien states that he found the source of his second novel in an old book from the church of Beauvais: "un des livres de l'aumeire / mon seignor saint Pere a Biavuez".[1]

The most evident example of this link between the fictional text and the book-object is obviously *Don Quixote*. Indeed, by parodying the earlier tradition of chivalric novels, Cervantes includes

DOI: 10.4324/9781003223641-2

and mirrors in his book all previous books of chivalric fiction. The Hidalgo de la Mancha "se daba a leer libros de caballerías, con tanta afición y gusto", to the point of turning his life into an imitation of the books he had read. In this sense, the novelistic character, insofar as the work that contains him establishes a new relationship between text and world, is often a reader-character: a hero whose actions are conditioned by some link to the book. Enide *was* the Virgilian book; she *read* it to the point that her life 'imitated' its *fictio*, in the same way that Don Quixote *was* the book of Rinaldo, of the Cid and of the other chivalric heroes he had read.

In the literary tradition, many famous characters embodied this topos of the 'double book': Dante's Francesca or Flaubert's Emma Bovary – fictional characters who mirrored themselves in the books they read. But the same narrative device is present throughout modern literature, for instance, in the 'bourgeois novel' developed in France in the second half of the seventeenth century. Here, the loves of the lawyers' daughters become subjects of fiction precisely because they are based on the 'misunderstandings' of a book, on the 'doubling' of a pre-existing book within the narrative text. In Antoine Furetière's *Roman borugeois* (1666), Javotte, the daughter of the lawyer Vollichon, reads the gallant, aristocratic novels of the early seventeenth century. Her sentimental education becomes 'imitative' of the books she has read, and the girl is thus presented in 'comic' contrast with the petit-bourgeois reality of her life. Javotte asks the never-failing gentleman: "je voudrais bien vous prier de me prêter le livre ou vous avez pris tout ce que vous avez dit".[2] By these words, Javotte makes it clear how much credibility books had in her life and what existential misunderstanding would ensue. Indeed, "il n'y avait pas un livre où tout ce qu'on disait dans la conversation fût écrit".[3] Finally the reading of *Astrea*'s loves – a real novel in the hands of the fictional character – inevitably leads Javotte to desire "qu'on lui fît l'amour dans les formes et à la manière du livre qui l'avait charmée".[4]

Similarly, in Stendhal's last unfinished novel (1839–1842), Lamiel, a young girl from a Norman village, abruptly removed from the orphanage to the salon of the Duchess of Miossens to be her reader, endangers her chances of knowing what love is precisely because books influence her life.

> Lamiel trouva sur l'étagère de livres l'*Histoire des quatre fils Aymon*. [...] elle oublia qu'il lui était défendu d'aller voir la danse [...]. Ce livre, confisqué par Hautemare à un écolier libertin, fit des ravages incroyables dans l'âme de la petite fille. [...] elle pensait que ce serait bien autre chose de se promener dans le cimetière, tout à côté de la danse, en donnant le bras à un des quatre fils Aymon.[5]

Of course, in Proust's *Recherche*, too, besides the fictitious books that the hero reads, such as Bergotte's, there is a very real book hidden within the text. However, in this case, the 'hidden book' is not exterior to the narrative but rather a shadow of Proust's own work, of its project, or more precisely, it is the expectation of the work in its book-form. "Moi, c'était autre chose que les adieux d'un mourant à sa femme que j'avais à écrire, de plus long et à plus d'une personne. Long à écrire" (*Le Temps retrouvé*).[6] Proust's 'bovarysm' thus evolves towards a self-referential sentiment: the frustration of Madame Bovary, her desire to live as in 'other people's books', becomes in Proust a paradoxical nostalgia[7] for his own book 'not yet written' – *long à écrire*.

Given its frequency, this relationship between the text one writes and the book one has read seems to have structural significance. It is not just a metaphor, but rather something that concerns the phylogeny of novelistic language. From his point of view, Albert Thibaudet clarified the problem in 1925: the French critic wanted to understand the identification processes, engendered by the narrative text, between the reader of novels and the fictional characters. A woman's bedroom, Thibaudet argued, becomes in the literary tradition the place where novels happen precisely because it is the place where novels are read, where the novels are experienced. The book of novels is therefore a book which wants to reproduce life, which wants to resemble it as much as possible, to the point of simulating its own existence in the lives of its characters. In other words, a book of novels includes its reading among the contents of its own representation, so that the character and the reader can be in a similar position: the novel is read in the same (or 'similar') room in which it takes place.[8]

This chapter will explore the concept of the 'fictional book'. Starting with some observations on the narrative manuscripts produced between the thirteenth and fourteenth centuries, we shall try to examine the image of the novelistic book in the modern literary tradition as it is reflected in the fictional text: indeed, the novel text and the book-object seem to influence each other.

2 Inside and outside the book

During the centuries in which vernacular literatures developed, the early manuscripts of courtly-chivalric fiction, that is, the first novels of Old French literature, displayed some recurring features.[9] Narrative texts were mostly collected in so-called miscellaneous codices. These are manuscripts that brought together several texts, copied in the same book according to internal relationships between one text and another. Indeed, the act of 'transcribing together', the act of 'collecting texts in the same book', is not a neutral operation. On the contrary, it sometimes reveals unexpected links between different works. These relationships between texts contained in the same book can often clarify the interpretation of the texts themselves and their uses in the cultural milieu that produced a specific miscellaneous book.[10] The *mise en recueil* ('collecting texts') – according to the French definition – thus became a literary case study. The large number of miscellaneous manuscripts that transmitted narrative works between the thirteenth and the fourteenth century confirms the relevance of this particular book-form. Furthermore, the fact that chivalric novels could develop into 'narrative cycles' – the Tristan cycle, the Lancelot cycle and so on – can also be explained through the material form of the miscellaneous book. In fact, this type of manuscript, because of its material features, made it possible to extend, continue and link texts together, until they formed a diegetic cycle.[11]

The well-known example of the Parisian manuscript BnF, fr. 1450 (thirteenth century) may clarify this kind of function. The book contains the *Roman de Troie*, an extensive narrative inspired by the defeat and exodus of the Trojans; the *Roman d'Eneas*, a rewriting of the Virgilian poem; and the *Brut*, a saga centred on the Trojans' arrival in Britain, including Arthur's kingdom. Furthermore, in the same manuscript, Chrétien de Troyes's five courtly and Arthurian novels follow this first series of texts. The narrative structure resulting from the combination of the different texts is very significant and allows for an overall interpretation of the entire book-object. In fact, going backwards: the reader of the Parisian manuscript moves from Chrétien's courtly and Arthurian setting to the pseudo-historical framework of that literary world thanks to the *Brut*, which narrates the events of the Bretons and Arthurian history. Then, from the *Brut* the reader can go back, through the *Roman d'Eneas*, to the Trojan framework, from which the Bretons claim to descend, assimilating themselves to Aeneas. Finally, from the *Roman d'Eneas* the reader returns to the origin with the *Roman de Troie*, the fall of Troy and the escape of its people. Therefore, an intertwined narrative structure develops beyond the single texts throughout the book.[12] The truly novelistic texts, namely Chrétien's five narratives, are thus enclosed within a 'context'. They are contained in a *before* and an *outside* of the novel; they are placed at the centre of an overall plot that the individual novels evoke but do not make explicit. Only the book-object, that is, the Parisian manuscript as a whole – and not the single texts – provides the continuous development of the story-line, the uninterrupted duration of the different narratives.

Another example, among many others, may concern the Vatican codex Reg. lat. 1522 (fourteenth century). This manuscript contains the *Roman de la rose*, a monumental oneiric-erotic narrative, and the *Tornoiment as dames de Paris*, a satirical tale of a fight between Parisian women. In this case, a bond concerning the incipit of the two texts links them to each other. Probably the two works are collected in the same book because both are accounts of a dream vision. "Maintes gens dient que en songes / n'a se fables non et mençonges" ('many people say that dreams are only fables and lies') in the incipit of the *Roman de la rose*; "ou soit de voir ou de mençonge / l'autre jor je songe un songe" ('whether true or false, the other day I had a dream') in the incipit of the *Tornoiment*. Therefore, the reader who wishes to explain the material connection of the two texts in the Vatican manuscript can use the means of intertextuality: the book links *Rose* and *Tornoiment* because its medieval scribe perceived a dreamlike narrating voice in both works.

Ultimately, these examples seem to confirm the preconception criticised by Barthes:[13] since its origins, the narrative book must connect, flow and last.

Given this miscellaneous and 'connective' tradition that distinguishes many medieval narrative books, it is perhaps useful to investigate the origins and development of this book-form. In fact, although from the thirteenth to the fourteenth century many narrative manuscripts were miscellanies, nevertheless before this period the same miscellaneous structure was used to transmit other kinds of texts, for example, historical or theological texts. Therefore, within this typology of manuscripts, we should identify a pertinent line of comparison that explains how the link between the book-form and the narrative text was formed. In other words, in the following pages we will ask whether there is a correspondence between the *mise en recueil*, as book structure, and the *conjointure*, as textual structure.[14]

'Composing', 'uniting', 'ordering' or 'putting together' different texts, different voices and their diegetic parts means making a narrative as if the text served to unify the articulation and the intrinsic plurality of the story. The same actions of 'composing' and 'ordering' delineate a very ancient stage of poetic evolution. Indeed, from its very beginnings narrative poetry had to resolve the dialectic between the unitary principle – for example, the inspiring Muse or the work in its completeness – and the multiple variety of stories, that is, the diversity of subjects and narrated facts. The dialectic between the unity of the narrative and the multiplicity of events constitutes a poetical archetype. In Homer, for instance, 'the Muse teaches the *stories*', strictly in the plural – οἴμασ Μοῦσ᾽ ἐδίδαξε.[15] And hence, the poet-narrator must develop these stories κατὰ κόσμον, 'according to an order'. That is, he must 'singularise' them, transform them into a single, unified narrative. Aeschylus considered his tragedies τεμάχη τῶν Ὁμήρου μεγάλων δείπνων, 'slices cut from Homer's great lunches', that is, sections of larger stories, individual scenes detached from a superior narrative continuity.[16]

These are very ancient examples that address the same problem that would also be faced by the moderns: how to represent, within the closed, unitary time and space of the text, the multiplicity and variety of 'life', of 'history', of the 'out-of-text',[17] where the narrated events took place? Homer's or Aeschylus's poetic statements raise the question of the relationship between the unity of the work, which arbitrarily establishes a beginning and a conclusion, and the unbegun, the unfinished, the 'before' of the story, its 'after', its 'during' and the 'elsewhere'. What happened before the narrated facts? What happened at the same time but elsewhere, or what will happen later? This range of problems defines the intrinsic variety of the existential matter that the narrative work seeks to represent.[18]

The classic rhetorical quarrel between *ordo naturalis* – the narrative that follows the natural causal chronology of events – and *ordo artificialis* – the textual plot that disregards 'natural time', altering the order of events by means of analexis and prolexis – is only a particular case of the overall problem. It is the same issue already expressed by Homer through the contrast between οἴμασ and κόσμον: on the one hand, the multiplicity and internal variety of stories coexisting in the Muse, and on the other, the closed, singular order of the narrative, which is the only possibility available to the poet. In short, the problem is that any narrator can represent in the diegesis only one event at a time, whereas in 'life' many different things can be perceived and spoken simultaneously.[19] Aristotle addressed this issue with regard to the unity of narrative: "many and indeed innumerable things [πολλὰ καὶ ἄπειρα] happen to an individual, some of which do not go to make up any unity" (*Poetics*, 8, 1451a 15–20). Erich Auerbach wrote on the same subject more than two millennia later: "life has always long since begun, and it is always still going on. And the people whose story the author is telling experience much more than he can ever hope to tell".[20] Therefore, the qualities of the narrative text derive from the millenary persistence of this problem: the search for those linguistic or compositional functions that should distort the textual linearity, allowing the simultaneous perception of a variety of facts – from the *ordo artificialis* to mimesis, from multilingualism to free indirect speech. These are inventions of narrative language, historically distinct but aimed at the same solution: the attempt to represent in the unitary fiction of the work – in the two-dimensional text – the multiple reality of the facts – that 'life long since begun and still going on', as Auerbach wrote, that is the *hors-texte* of every narration.

Compared to the unitary force of the narrative (Homeric κόσμον), the 'out-of-text' represents the actual realm of the random, the sphere of the possible and the multiple that characterises life, that is, the ultimate target of any realistic representation. It is by imitating the varying and manifold *outside* that the novel constructs its particular textuality, and the novelistic book will thus be able to simulate its interaction with life 'out-of-the-book'.

Throughout its development as a literary genre, the novel has never renounced the attempt to include the 'out-of-text' in the narrative, to recall it within the book, thus producing a dialectic between the perception of life and historicity, placed at the fringes of the text, and the pure diegetic *fictio*, placed inside the text. Let us take a simple example from Balzac, who is obviously a model for such osmosis between text and reality – increased, moreover, by the overall architecture of the *Comédie*. In the novel *Albert Savarus* (1842), the moral qualities of the eponymous protagonist, now nearing the tragic climax of his story, are judged, Balzac says, by a 'man who later became one of the most prominent personalities of Besançon', "qui depuis est devenu l'une des capacités de Besançon".[21]

> Cette profession de foi, cette déclaration d'ambitieux [...] fut, au dire du seul homme capable de juger Savarus et qui depuis est devenu l'une des capacités de Besançon, un chef-d'œuvre d'adresse, de sentiment, de chaleur, d'intérêt et de séduction.

However, Balzac does not tell us who the man is who expresses such a judgement on Albert Savarus. Have we already met him in the novel? Or perhaps it is a statement of (pseudo-)reality expressed by the narrator? – as if the story of Savarus, beyond the text in which Balzac invented it, really happened in Besançon, so much so that other people judged it. About the man who made such a judgement on the fictional protagonist, Balzac says above all that 'he later became an important person', but the story makes no further mention of him. A question therefore arises. When? At what moment will this man become an important person? After the text, outside the novel? If, therefore, this man coincides with one of the book's characters surrounding Savarus's story, we should have the impression – which is usual in Balzac – that the events of those characters continue beyond the text, that the fictional persons have a continuation, a duration, outside the novel. If, on the other hand – as some exegetical notes speculate – by that allusion Balzac had paid homage to a real, historical man, namely, a friend of his from Besançon,[22] the paradox would still remain.[23] Indeed, within the narrative *fictio*, we would have the judgement formulated by a real and historical individual on the life of a fictional character, and furthermore this would take place in a 'synchronic' way: the real individual would be present in the events of the fictional character. In both cases, an *outside* – 'outside the novel' or 'outside, in reality' – enters the interior of the work. Through this exchange, between the *outside* and the *inside*, the novel displays its realist claims on textual temporality, that is, the possibility that the text simulates a chronic relationship with 'the life still going on' – *qui depuis est devenu* – of which Auerbach spoke.

These functions of novelistic language began to appear in some medieval narratives. Here, in the medieval literary tradition, the textual device that allows this kind of exchange between the book and the *outside* can emerge as a 'narrative metalepsis'. According to Genette's description, the metalepsis "consiste à feindre que le poète opère lui-même les effets qu'il chante [...], comme [...] lorsque Diderot [...] écrit dans *Jacques le fataliste*: 'Qu'est-ce qui m'empêcherait de *marier* le Maître ...?'", and Genette then defines its rhetorical functions as "toute intrusion du narrateur ou du narrataire extradiégétique dans l'univers diégétique".[24]

In Old French literature, between the twelfth and thirteenth centuries, we can observe metalepsis in Renaut de Beaujeu's *Bel inconnu*. In terms of plot, this text is a chivalric narrative about the exploits of a young hero hesitating between two different loves. But actually the *Bel inconnu* is a quite mysterious work, and one could say that the narrative deals with the mimesis of its own fiction, its diegesis representing its own writing, and questioning its status as a 'closed book'.[25] With regard to the plot structure, after freeing two women held captive separately, the hero of *Bel inconnu*, called Guinglain – though at the beginning of the story he does not know his name – is held back by the first woman and then by the other; both of them wish to marry him. The knight's desire, especially in its sensual connotations, seems to prefer the first woman, a fairy *pucelle*. However, at the end of the novel, Guinglain will marry the other, the second woman, by order of Arthur and by courtly custom. Added to these two female characters is the presence of a third woman, whom the narrator addresses on several occasions and who appears as the novelist's beloved and the implicit reader of the entire work – which is in fact dedicated to her. The ending of *Bel inconnu*, with the full manifestation of the beloved-reader, is a great metalepsis, of both author and reader.[26]

Ci faut li roumans et define.
Bele, vers cui mes cuers s'acline,
Renals de Biauju molt vos prie

[...]
Quant vos plaira, dira avant,
u il se taira ore et tant.
Mais por un biau sanblant mostrer
vos feroit Guinglain retrover
s'amie, que il a perdue,
qu'entre ses bras le tenroit nue.
Se de çou li faites delai,
si ert Guinglains en tel esami
que ja mais n'avera s'amie.
D'autre vengeance n'a il mie,
mais por la soie grant grevance
ert sor Guinglain ceste vengeance,
que ja mais jor n'en parlerai
tant que le bel sanblant avrai.

[Here ends the novel. Fair lady, to whom my heart submits, Renaut de Beaujeu most humbly prays you [...]. When you wish, he will tell further or else be silent forever. If you show him a gracious countenance, he will make Guinglain find his lost beloved – and hold her naked in his arms. But if you delay in granting him this, Guinglain must bear great distress, because he will never find his beloved again. He [the narrator, Renaut] has no other vengeance, and for his great sorrow this vengeance will fall on Guinglain – of whom I will never tell again until you grant me your favour].

The narrator, through an ambiguous interplay between first and third person, concludes the work by stating that he could continue the knight's story, and even reverse the epilogue, should his lady-reader show him a sign of love. Indeed, the narrator could return his hero to the first woman, the fairy *pucelle* – Guinglain's true desire – and thus remove him from the second woman, whom he has just married. The beloved-reader is involved in the potential of the text: by showing her sympathy for the narrator, she can induce him to continue the story; whereas, for the moment, the narrator avenges his 'true love', for the reader herself, by handing Guinglain over to the less desired woman. The narrator and the reader, as in Genette's metalepsis, are thus able to act directly in the development of the novel, breaking through the boundary that separates text from reality.

Yet, the entry of the 'out-of-text' in *Bel inconnu* seems to produce the opposite result of Balzac's novel. If in *Albert Savarus*, the *outside* entered the story, increasing the sense of reality: the man from Besançon would have a continuing existence irrespective of the novelistic book; by contrast, in the Old French text the narrator's confession – 'if the reader wants it, I will give a sequel to my hero's story' – reaffirms the status of fiction. The novel, says Renaut at the end of *Bel inconnu*, does not exist outside its invention, and precisely because it lacks a real reference, it can be continued, expanded and twisted through an exchange of narrative desire between narrator and reader. In short, Balzac's 'simulated reality' achieves a greater degree of realism than the 'real possibility' (that the story continues) expressed in *Bel inconnu*. Therefore, we may note that the fragments of reality that the novel disseminates on the fringes of the text – between the 'inside of the book' and the 'outside of life' – do not always produce the same effects. While such realist, or pseudo-realist, insertions serve to demonstrate the relationship between the work and the world, they can also lead in diametrically opposite directions. On the one hand, they increase the perception of identity between text and life, as happens in Balzac, and on the other hand, they explicitly display the narrative fiction, as in *Bel inconnu*. In the latter case, the clear admission in the epilogue that the novel is a *fictio* seems to contradict the rules of nineteenth-century Realism, the Realism of Henry James, for example: "certain accomplished novelists have a habit of giving themselves away"; this kind of novelist "in a digression, a parenthesis or an aside, [...] admits that the events he narrates have not really happened, and that he can give his narrative any turn the reader may like best".[27] James condemned an authorial attitude of this kind, as threatening the "impression of reality" that a writer should always pursue through the mimesis of existence. For the American novelist, this mimesis consisted in reproducing, within the text, "life *without* rearrangement",[28] that is, as mentioned above, a restitution of variety, the multiple and existential randomness.

But, actually, for the purposes of our analysis – which concerns the image of the fictional book and its reality 'out-of-text' – in *Bel inconnu* the mirroring of the *fictio* outside the book is not explained – in Jamesian fashion – by the inexperience of the writer. Instead, the Old French text produces those effects intuited by Thibaudet. That is, the aim of the narration in *Bel inconnu* is to bring the reader and the fictional character together in the 'same room'. To appreciate this level of 'extra-textuality', let us return to the plot of the novel. In moving between the two women, it happens that Guinglain, already betrothed to the second woman, spends a night with the first one, the fairy girl. That night, in his attempt to reach the bedroom, the knight falls victim to some spells – cast by the fairy herself. Finally in the bedroom, the fairy *pucelle* reveals all her powers to him: "or vos dirai, se vos volés, / en quel maniere et coment / jo sai faire l'encantement", 'now I will tell you, if you wish, how and why I know how to cast the spell' (vv. 4930–4932). After telling him about all the magical arts she learnt since childhood, the girl, desired by Guinglain, continues as follows:

> Si sai tos encantemens fare,
> deviner, et conoistre en l'are
> quanques dou mois puet avenir.
> [...]
> et saciés que molt a lonc tens
> qu'amer vos començai premiers.
> Ains que vos fuissiés chevaliers
> vos amai je [...].
> Ce so ge tot premierement
> l'aventure certainnement
> que vos avés ici trovee
> et tote vostre destinee.
> Je resavoie par mon sens
> qu'a la cort venrïés par tens.
> Biaus amis, certes, *je sui cele
> qui* fis savoir a la pucele
> qui estoit apielee Helie
> qu'a la cort alast querre aïe
> [...]
> *Et si sui cele*, biaus amis,
> quant eüstes Mabon ocis
> et quant le Fier Baissier fasistes,
> la vois que vos aprés oïstes,
> qui vostre non vos fis savoir,
> ço fui je, biaus amis, por voir,
> por vos faire souef ester,

dormir et la nuit reposer
[...].
Sacié molt *me sui entremisse
en tos sanblans, en tos servisse*
(vv. 4945–5006; italics added)

[That is why I can cast any spell; I can foresee and predict whatever may happen. [...] You must know that I have loved you for a long time; before you became a knight, I already loved you [...]. I knew in advance, for certain, the adventure you found here and your whole destiny. I knew by my wisdom that you would go to the court [of Arthur]. My dear friend, *it was I who* told Helie, the maiden, to go to court to ask for help [...]. And, my dear friend, when you killed Mabon and then gave the 'Fearsome Kiss', *it was I who was* the voice you heard – who made your name known to you. It was really me, and I did it to reassure you, to make you sleep and rest during the night. [...] You must know that *I was involved in all the events and in every solution*]

In her confession, the fairy girl claims her role in everything that has happened to the knight; indeed, the *pucelle* summarises every adventure the hero has had so far (*ce so ge tot premierement l'aventure*, 'I knew the adventure in advance'), offers us the novel's analepsis, and claims responsibility for it: *je suis celle qui* [...] 'I am the one who carried the story forward'. As some critics have observed,[29] the impression that 'the I of the girl' reflects a 'narrating I' – the one who organises the plot – arises immediately. She who managed every action of the diegesis thus becomes a figure of the ongoing text. Guinglain, in the room of the *pucelle*, is in effect in the presence of 'his' book, in front of his own novel – or at least a part of it, the part that has unfolded up to that moment. From this perspective, the novel's ending also assumes a clearer meaning. Returning Guinglain to the fairy *pucelle* – as the narrator hypothesises in his conclusion[30] – returning him to *celle qui* [...], to the *voix*, to the one who told[31] and carried the whole story forward, actually means returning the character to his narrative writing – of which marriage to the other woman would mark a momentary end.[32]

The reader of *Bel inconnu*, together with the hero of the novel, witnesses the encounter with 'his own book'; for a moment, they both find themselves reading the 'same' novel. The room where the knight meets the *pucelle*, his *woman-book* – as Enide was for her husband – and the room where the reader reads the novel overlap with each other. We end up reading about the knight who 'reads' our own book: namely, the book that the *pucelle*-narrator is writing for us and for the fictional hero. In this regard, what Blanchot wrote about the Homeric sirens seems fitting – that they were a textual mirror of the ongoing narrative: "réunir dans un même espace Achab et la baleine, les Sirènes et Ulysse, voilà le vœu secret qui fait d'Ulysse Homère, d'Achab Melville [...], hélas un livre, rien qu'un livre".[33] It would thus be the 'secret wish' of any narrative to bring together, to conjoin, the character and his book. Their intersection, arranged on the diegetic plane in an apparently ordinary way, obviously transvalues the reader's position, since his reading overlaps with the character's reading of his own story: "il n'est pas vraiment lecteur. Il est la lecture: le mouvement par lequel le livre se communique à lui-même".[34] The outcomes of these narrative operations is 'bovarysm' in the deepest sense (that in which Flaubert *is* Madame), the paradoxical nostalgia for the never-lived; the result is identification with a literary character whose exemplarity will be false, disappointing or frustrating, because actually the narrative character is a copy, an image, of the reading Self. Ultimately, these would be the psychological consequences produced in the 'novel reader' when he discovers the outside-image of his book reflected inside the text.[35]

3 The multiplicity of the real and the randomness of the book

As we have mentioned, these interactions between the reader-character and his book often occur in the course of the regular development of the diegetic plane – the sequence of narrative actions. Indeed, as Barthes pointed out, the novel entails a programmatic rejection of metalanguage.[36] That is, novelistic language in principle cannot split into two different linguistic systems: on the one hand a narrating language, and on the other a self-reflecting language. According to Barthes, even the self-reflexive function, if it is active, must operate as a diegetic development. That is, it must be part of the 'story', producing, at most, a level of pseudo-diegesis.[37] Therefore, it is no coincidence that the *pucelle*, the *book-woman* of *Bel inconnu*, claims for herself a complete continuity *en tos sanblans, en tos servisse*, in all the events of the story: *je me suis entremise*, 'I was present', 'there I was'. In other words, she acts in the diegesis of the novel (*sanblans* and *servisse*), in the sequence of its actions, ultimately in the multiplicity and randomness of the narrative facts. From the point of view of *fictio*, the stories – the manifold set of events – and the book, οἴμασ and κόσμον, both belong to the diegetic variety. That is, the narrated facts and the book that reflects them both participate equally in the fiction of the narrative universe: the book-object is no less fictional than the text it contains.

Erich Köhler addressed a similar issue through the category of 'novelistic chance' – *Der literarische Zufall*, 'coincidence in Literature'.[38] Köhler wondered: why, in Alfred de Musset's *Confession* (1836), does Octave happen to drop a fork under the table so that, when he bends down to pick it up, he discovers his mistress playing footsie with another man? Why does such a random occurrence happen – among the range of all possibilities? By virtue of this sheer coincidence, Octave falls ill with the "maladie du siècle"[39] (a melancholy and perverse love), which will then serve as the narrative centre of the novel. From a structural point of view, we could reiterate the same kind of questions about any 'system of causes' in any 'realistic novel'. For example, in Balzac's *Duchesse de Langeais*, why does Armand de Montriveau, a former Napoleonic colonel, hardened by defeat and ill at ease in the face of the blandishments of the Bourbon Restoration, end up conversing with the Duchess of Langeais, who was by contrast "pleine de sentiments élevés, mais manquante d'une pensée qui les coordonnât"?[40] The development of the plot in Balzac's novel mainly comes from this accidental circumstance: by virtue of this randomness, Montriveau, a sombre soldier, allows his vanity to lead him into the abyss of coldly calculating seduction.

Köhler begins by denying that chance appears in the plots of novels simply because it is present in life and consequently should be present in fiction "which, in some way, is always mimetic" and thus obliged to represent the random variety of events[41]. On the contrary, he argues, 'novelistic chance' performs the function of representing a necessity, an individual destiny: Octave as 'the child of the Century' in the *Confession*. However, this destiny must emerge from a common, possible existential plane, as a reflection of the multiplicity and *varietas* existing in life: as happens to Octave, everyone can drop a fork. From this perspective, the relationship between novel and chance becomes a structural feature. That is, it concerns the aesthetic level of representation: "chance arbitrarily crosses an intentional act, provides a necessity and reveals it as a realised possibility. Literature is not only subject to this dialectic [being mimesis], but also constitutes its object", since the novel is an "instrument of mediation [...] between art and reality"[42] – just as chance is an instrument of mediation between the possible and the necessary. By means of such considerations, Köhler raised the problem of a *principium individuationis* within the novel, that is, the problem of a linguistic and narrative relationship between the text and its varying and multiple *outside*. From these arguments Köhler derived the idea of the novel as a 'necessary form of randomness',[43] that is, a narrative language able to channel into the uniqueness of a diegetic chance 'many and innumerable things' that constitute the extra-textual life of the characters (πολλὰ καὶ ἄπειρα, according to Aristotle).

In medieval literature, one of the most striking images of the 'fictional book' as an object-container of the multiple and various appears in the cycle of *Lancelot*, namely in the first pages of the *Estoire del saint Graal*, that is, at the incipit of the entire novelistic cycle. The narrator of *Estoire*, speaking in the first person, relates the genesis of his book as a concrete object. He claims that the novel we read has been physically delivered to him by Christ in the form of a very small booklet. Christ himself then asked the narrator to read and copy that small book.

> me prist par le main destre et si me mist dedens un *petit livret* [...], si commenchai a lire [...]. Et quant je oi gardé tant ke ja estoit prime passee, si me fui avis ke je n'i avoie rien leü, tant i avoit encore a lire, car je i vi tant de letre ke je en fui tous esbahis comment *si grans plentés de paroles* pooit estre amonchelee en si *petit livret*, qui n'estoit pas au mien avis plus lons ne plus les en nule guise ke est une paume. Si m'en merveillai tant que je en mescreïsse moi meïsme qui le veoie, se chil ne le m'eüst baillié qui *grant plenté de choses* puet metre en *petit de lieu*.[44]

> [he took me by the right hand and put a *small book* in it [...], I began to read [...]. And when I held it in my hand for the whole of the prime hour, it seemed to me that I had read nothing,

because there was still much to read. In fact, I saw so many letters in it that I wondered deeply that *so many words* could accumulate in such a *small booklet* – in my opinion no longer or wider than the palm of my hand. And I was so astonished that I would have doubted that I had actually seen it, had it not been given to me by One who knows how to put *so many things* into so *little space*.]

The 'little book' that the writer receives from Christ and begins to read is a strange narrative that includes the narrator's 'family novel' – "commenchemens de ton linaige", 'the beginning of your lineage' – and then other titles, all contained in this 'small book', which, by their inner diversity, clearly express a logic of narrative multiplicity. Or rather, since it is the book written by Christ, a logic of narrative universality: 'then, I found a title that said: *Here begins the Book of the Holy Grail*. [...] I found another title that said: *Here is the beginning of Fears*. [...] I found the fourth title that said: *Here begins the Marvellous*'.

The image of the 'little book' thus determines an opposition between the multiplicity of the stories written down and contained in the manuscript and the minuscule dimensions of the book-object: an opposition between the *grant plenté des choses* (the narrative variety) and the *petit livret* (the small book that contains it). The manuscript from which the writer copies his novel thus looks like a 'miraculous miscellaneous book'. Its miscellaneous form is obviously a metaphor for the 'universal book', that is, the divine writing able to collect, by means of its necessity, all the varying and random things existing 'outside the book'. Indeed, the manuscript of the *Estoire* represents, within the text, its own book-form: the book in which *Lancelot-Graal*'s great narrative begins – the 'book of all stories' – reproduces in itself its own image, that is, the image of a miscellaneous book.[45]

In the seventeenth century, we find a very similar topos, but with a contrary meaning, in Furetière's *Roman bourgeois*.

> Si vous vous attendez, Lecteur, que ce livre soit la suite du premier, et qu'il y ait une connexité necessaire entr'eux, vous estes pris pour duppe. [...] Ce sont de *petites histoires et advantures arrivées en divers quartiers de la ville, qui n'ont rien de commun ensemble*, et que je tasche de rapprocher les unes des autres

autant qu'il m'est possible. Pour le soin de la liaison, je le laisse à *celuy qui reliera le livre*.

[If you hope, my reader, that this book is a sequel to the first one and that there is a necessary continuity between the two parts, you have been duped. [...].These are *stories and adventures that occurred in different points of the city, they have nothing in common with each other*, and I try to link them together as much as possible. I commit their connection to *he who will bind the book*.] (italics added)

These two examples, the *Estoire* and the *Roman bourgeois* – each according to its own 'book culture' – show us how the text of a novel aims to include within its representation its own material form and how the book of novels enacts a dialectic between text and book-object. La *grant plenté de choses* (*Estoire*) or *les petites histoires qui n'ont rien de commun ensemble* (*Roman bourgeois*) represent the varying and multiple 'out-of-the-book', which the text includes within its narrative. Moreover, even in the *Roman bourgeois*, the book-form – its material binding – is mentioned by Furetière as the only reason for the novel's unity: the bookbinder would be solely accountable for all the 'little stories' being collected together in the same volume. What Christ did in the *petit livret* of the *Estoire* – that is, collecting all the stories into one manuscript – is now the task of a bookseller in Furetière's novel.

4 The novel's incipit: rewriting the book and rewriting the history

The multiplicity and variety that characterise the 'narratable matter' – the life, *before* and *outside* its arrangement in the text – can thus interact with the image of the novelistic book.

In the more traditional forms of the modern novel, we can observe this hierarchy between the multiple *outside* and the *inside* of the novel's text as the recreation of exterior randomness, according to Köhler's analysis. Following the German philologist, we can observe, for instance, that de Musset's *Confession* begins by distinguishing the voice of the initial narrator from the 'I' of the character, Octave, who relates his 'exemplary illness' in the first person: "Pour écrire l'histoire de sa vie, il faut d'abord avoir vécu; aussi n'est-ce pas la mienne que j'écris". This incipit marks a preliminary 'out-of-the-novel', that is, an apparent opposition of voices: on the one hand 'the writer', extraneous to diegetic events, and on the other 'the one who lived them'. After this statement, the novel sketches out its historiographical context, a 'clarification' of the History and epoch within which the events concerning Octave will unfold: de Musset describes the collapse of the heroic generation, the failure of the heirs of the Napoleonic era. It is therefore a second 'out-of-the-novel', concerning the causal and contextual *outside* of the narrative. In these historiographical pages, the text represents the historical multiplicity, that is, that diversity of cases and events that remain at the novel's fringes: "Pendant les guerres de l'empire...". Only at this point does Octave take the floor directly to "raconter *à quelle occasion je fus* pris d'abord de la maladie du siècle". The *occasion*, among the many chances evoked by the *outside*, is the event that allows the enunciation in the first person (*je fus pris...*), it is proper novelistic chance; it opens the novel's time, including itself in the previous historical and collective chronology: "des *milliers d'enfants* se regardaient entre eux", but only Octave will emerge as *enfant du siècle*. The *Confession* then closes with a further break: suddenly Octave's 'I' stops narrating, and the last chapter is related in the third person – perhaps by the same voice that in the incipit claimed itself extraneous to the events of the story. In short, de Musset's montage circumscribes the 'novel of Octave' between two *outsides* – the first concerning the historical and narrative time, the second concerning the different narrating voices, and thus one enters the novel and one exits from it. Upstream there is the 'time of History' and downstream the 'time of the narrator'. Ultimately, this narratological framework is very traditional; its assumptions are not substantially different from those that in the thirteenth century organised a narrative book in the form of a miscellany. The 'book of de Musset' establishes the 'contextual relations' of the novel: its *before*, its *outside*, that is, the thresholds of entry and exit, as was the case in several medieval narrative manuscripts – for instance, we saw it in the Parisian fr. 1450. De Musset introjects into the text what was not a textual but a book structure – which originally served to keep the novelistic space in contact with the multiplicity of its *hors-texte*. De Musset thus not only writes a novel but also ends up narrativising – more or less consciously – the form of an old 'novelistic book'.

All things considered, the progressive introjection of the book-object into the narrative text is one of the most significant achievements of the nineteenth-century novel. Between de Musset and Proust – the novel placed between two thresholds (de Musset) and the book that narrates the awaiting itself (Proust) – an 'intermediate' solution can be observed in Gérard de Nerval. In *Sylvie* (1853), the dreamy first-person narration of a return to Valois, to the places and impressions of youth, closes on a chapter entitled 'Last Sheet', "Dernier Feuillet". Here, by this title and its content, suddenly the *fictio* of the diegesis, that is, the semi-oneiric action of the narrative character, achieves the concrete physicality of the book – its last sheet of paper – and the hero is then absorbed into its narrator, that is, the writer of the *dernier feuillet*. In that ending, the self of diegesis approaches the narrating self:[46] "Telles sont les chimères qui charment et égarent au matin de la vie. *J'ai essayé de les fixer* sans beaucoup d'ordre".[47] Thus, compared to the 'book of de Musset', 'Nerval's book' – whose exit threshold juxtaposes the character and the narrator: he who experienced the chimeras and he who wrote them down – is more included and more involved in the diegesis of the novel. The book-object is narrativised, by virtue of the juxtaposition of the hero and the writer of the story. However, compared to the 'book of Proust', coextensive with all its voices, the 'book of Nerval' still separates, albeit internally within the text, the times of its different enunciations: first, the one who acts and then the one who writes[48] – who 'fixes in writing' (*j'ai essayé de les fixer*).

During the twelfth and thirteenth centuries, when the earliest forms of the narrative book were produced, the still germinal stage of these problems did not allow the dialectic between the *outside* of the book and the *inside* of the story to be resolved by the modern devices of textual autonomy – that is, by the narrative solutions we have just observed in some nineteenth-century novels. In the early centuries, this relationship took place on a level just beyond that of mere textuality, that is, on the level of the manuscript-object and the book-form. Moreover, simultaneously, the same dialectic was prolonged through the use of *mise en abyme*: that is, it was embodied by some narrative figures, namely by the book-character – Enide and the *pucelle* of *Bel inconnu* – or by the textual doubling of the book-form, with the 'miraculous collection' of the *petit livret*, the inner copy of the cyclical-miscellaneous book of *Lancelot-Graal*. In both cases, the purpose was to represent the image of the ongoing relationship between the novel and its *outside*: a duration between the *inside* of the novelistic narration and the *outside* of the narratable, multiple and varying – in short, between the novel and History.

From this point of view, that is, from the perspective of a pragmatics of text and book, the relationship between fictional *inside* and historical *outside* seems to overturn the Aristotelian assumption (*Poetics*, 9, 1451b): the idea that historiography enunciates the 'things that have happened' [γενόμενα], while the discourse of *fictio* enunciates the 'things that might happen' [οἷα ἂν γένοιτο]. By virtue of its features of multiplicity, variety and randomness, it is rather the 'out-of-the-text' – History – that presents itself as the realm of 'what might happen'; whereas the *inside* unity of the *fictio* presents itself, within the book, as the realm of the 'happened'. That is, it singularises the multiplicity and variety of the 'out-of-the-text' on a single plane of action. The basic structure of 'de Musset's book' clearly shows this: among all the narrative possibilities contained in the *milliers d'enfants* – evoked in the novel's incipit, in its 'historiographical pages' – it is only Octave who singularises himself as an *enfant du siècle*. His *fictio* has 'happened' and is unique, while the other *milliers d'enfants* remain on the *outside* – multiple and possible.[49] This is the usual metonymic-metaphorical relationship between novel and History, between the *inside* and the *outside* of the book: "the (metaphorical) insight that every life is both 'like every other' at the same time 'utterly unique'".[50] However, from a pragmatic perspective, it is the novel text that claims, in its *inside*, the 'utterly unique life' and 'the happened', while 'every other similar life' remains in the random and possible exterior of History – as in de Musset's *Confession*. Solely from this point of view can we fully understand the question that Barthes asked of the novel as textual language: "pourquoi cette histoire-là parmi tant d'autres? [...] Pourquoi cette histoire plutôt qu'une autre?"[51] However idiosyncratic or naive it may appear, this question is actually perfectly appropriate, since it underlines the problem between the book and its *outside*, namely between the internal uniqueness of the novelistic diegesis – *cette histoire-là* – and the *outside* multiplicity, or rather the plurality of historical possibilities – *parmi tant d'autres*.

Now, we should consider that the book as a concrete object is the novel's main articulation towards the reality. That is, the book is the most evident outwardness of the text; it is the first *outside* of the text, since it belongs to the objects of the world, to its multiplicity and exteriority. Yet, as we have seen, it can reappear *inside*, simulating being involved in the diegetic representation. If the book appears in the text, mixed up with external objects – *parmi tant d'autres* – the *outside* and the *inside* switch, and the actual reality – that of the reader 'outside the novel' who is reading the book – is absorbed into the *fictio*. Finding himself somehow 'inside the book', the reader – who should not have forgotten that he is real – will be induced to recognise *cette histoire-là* – the *fictio* which includes 'his' book – as the closest to the reality he is experiencing. In this sense, the novel can generate identification with not only the characters, the events, the represented situations – according to its most usual functions – but can also generate a deeper identification with its structure. When the latter is at stake, the book-form is often involved.

A book that collects several texts, that is, the 'miscellaneous book', is obviously a formal structure within which the relationship between 'this story' and 'the other stories' can reverberate beyond the single text. In the thirteenth century, the example of the manuscript Arsenal 3516 (Paris, Bibliothèque de l'Arsenal) is illuminating. It is a codex, dating from around 1268, that reveals – at the highest level in the Old French tradition – the very idea of the miscellaneous book.[52] The codex contains more than 60 texts, belonging to different genres: from hagiographic tales to some works on calendars and the computation of time, from texts of courtly ethics to historiography, and finally including some narrative works – in verse and prose. In particular, the Arsenal manuscript is the only codex we have for the novel *Cristal et Clarie*, in octosyllabic verses, and the incomplete *Roman de Reinbert*, in prose. The relationship that both narratives texts entail with the book-form that contains them influences the very reading of the works.

The former relates the adventures of Cristal, in search of Clarie, an unknown woman who has appeared to him in a dream and of whose existence the hero is convinced. The *quête* for this woman organises the entire tale – along a somewhat 'schlerotic' diegetic plane, given its paratactic repetition of dozens of adventures. No wonder that the narrative, which is a novel of chivalry and love, opens on a courtly doctrine; the first 400 verses are in fact a didactics of amorous behaviour, summarising all the precepts of *courtoisie*:[53] from the phenomenology of lovesickness to the trials of refinement to which the lover is subjected. It is in the light of this courtly ideology that Cristal's *quête* will begin – after a night dream has made him fall in love with Clarie. However, the novel's point of interest lies more in that didactic and ideological incipit than in the events of the plot.[54] In fact, the courtly doctrine expressed at the beginning is not an original piece of writing, composed at the same time as the novel; instead, it consists of the addition of a pre-existing text within the novel, namely the insertion of Robert de Blois's *D'Amour*, a thirteenth-century treatise on courtly love precepts. The relationship between the novel and this love doctrine – extracted from another text and placed in the narrative's incipit – could be resolved in terms of evident intertextuality, or maybe in terms of an extreme example of the art of medieval quotation. However, the issue is complicated by the fact that *D'Amour* itself appears in the Arsenal manuscript a few pages before the novel (294v–295v); therefore, its duplication, or its 'plagiarism', within the codex should be explained by some inner and deeper reason. The reading effect goes beyond the limits of intertextuality or quotation;[55] rather, the reader of the Arsenal manuscript finds himself rereading within the novel of *Cristal et Clarie* the text that, a few pages earlier, he has already read 'outside the novel'. The treatise on love by Robert de Blois, a very real book, already existing in the 'reader's library' and in his memory, thus falls into the fictional universe of the novel.

Moreover, when the hero finally reaches Clarie – as he had dreamed in the incipit – and sexually possesses her against her will, actually raping her,[56] the reader may suspect that the courtly doctrine expressed in *D'Amour* is substantially overturned and that the amorous *quête* was nothing more than lust and sexual searching.[57] Clarie herself, after her rape, first reproaches the hero for his brutality – "Or avés fais tos vos talens, / est ce vos nus amendemens?" (vv. 8383–8384), 'now that you have satisfied yourself, are you better off?' – but then ends up desiring her sexual fulfilment rather than the liturgies of courtly love – "Faites tot vo plaisir de moi, / a vos me doins, a vos m'otroi" (vv. 8711 – 8712), 'take from me all your pleasure, I give you myself, I offer you myself'. In the novel, sexuality disinhibits and distorts the characters to the point that, when her father wants to make sure she is not in the room with a man, Claire accuses him of desiring sexual contact with her: "vos avés itel talant / de gesir ovoec vostre enfant. / Pechies est qu'hon de tel eage / s'entremet mais de tel putage" (vv. 8915–8918), 'you have desire to lie with your daughter; it is shameful that an old man should engage in such prostitution'. Courtly values – their rules of practice and language – are definitely overturned, becoming an explicit triumph of sexual phantasms.

From the point of view of textual and book pragmatics, the treatise *D'Amour*, which the reader had already read 'outside the novel', is thus included, and reread, 'inside the novel', only to be contradicted by the diegetic facts. This 'real and non-fictional book' and its ethical contents are thus reduced to ideological fantasy and courtly invention because in fact Cristal and Clarie are mirrors of much more 'realistic' behaviours than those codified by the didactics of the courtly treatise. By rewriting within it that book already existing in the external reality of the manuscript, the novel thus falsifies it, since the narrative belies on the diegetic level the behavioural pretensions of the treatise. The book *D'Amour*, its teaching about love, falls 'inside the novel' and becomes *fictio* and unreality, while the verisimilitude of the novel is doubled. On the one hand, the novelistic text reflects within itself the book which exists 'outside the novel', and on the other it represents, in the diegesis, the 'true reality' of erotic desire as opposed to the 'unrealistic' ideology of the treatise. The 'book *D'Amour*' thus emerges as doubly 'false': both because it is included in the narrative *fictio* and because it is narratively belied in its content.

Whoever produced the manuscript Arsenal 3516 seems to have been deeply interested in this kind of exchange between novel-text and its book-form, since he reiterates the relationship even further. In its last folios, the codex transmits the *Reinbert*, an unfinished chivalric narrative in prose.[58] Here the relationship between the novel and the book containing it takes place under the banner of 'historicity'. The *Roman de Reinbert* – in the part of the text we know – relates the adventures of its hero, the nephew of a Roman emperor, in the Eastern lands. Reinbert, a knight from the "terre de Pannone qui ore est apelee Hongrie", one night has a dream that seems to foreshadow the success of his exploits; he therefore sets off on adventure, moving from Eastern Europe to India. This is the novel's incipit:

60 *Books of stories and books of novels*

Segnor et dames, el commencement des regnes, quant nom furent mis es terres par les Grieus, sachiés que France fu premièrement nomee Gale, trusques a l'an ke li siecles avoit duré .v. m. ans et .vi. c. et xxiiiiii. ans. C'est l'an de l'incarnation Nostre Segnor . iii. c. ans et lxvi; ans, que Valentiniens estoit emperes de Rome. Tresqu'a cel jor, n'ot onques esté rois en France, mais il avoient .iii. conestables que il clamoient dus, et cil troi furent chievetaigne et conduisoient les François. Li uns ot nom Marchomerus, de la lignie al roi Priant de Troies; li autres od nom Sumon, de la lignie Anthenor, et li tiers Genelaus. Tot troi erent halt home et de moult grant poissance. Marchomerus ot un fil qui od nom Faramons, pros chevaliers estoit, fors et durs as armes et de grant vaillance. Quant Marchomerus fu mors, li Franc par commun esgart firent roi de Faramon; et si le coronerent l'an de l'incarnation Nostre Segnor Jhesu Crist .cccc. et xviii ans. Et dont estoit Theodosius empereres de Rome. Il avint si que Theodosius avoit un sien neveu qui moult estoit beax chevaliers et fors et adurés et entreprenans de tote riens ou il son honor savoit. Cil chevaliers tint la terre de Pannone qui ore est apelee Hongrie, et li chevaliers fu només Reinbers. Cil Reinbers songa une nuit ke il cachoit un lion qui tot estoit d'or, et si le prist, ce li fu avis. Al matin, quant il se fu levés ...

[Lords and ladies, at the beginning of the kingdoms, when the Greeks gave names to the lands, know that France was called Gaul, until the year of Creation 5626, which is the year 366 of the Incarnation of Our Lord, when Valentinian was Emperor of Rome. Until that day, there were no kings in France, but three *connétables* called dukes, and these three were captains and led the French. One was called Marcomerus, from the lineage of King Priam of Troy, the other was called Sumon, from the lineage of Antenor, the third Genelaus; all three were strong and powerful men. Marcomerus had a son whose name was Pharamond – he was a valiant knight, strong, skilled in arms and valorous. When Marcomerus died, the Franks commonly elected Pharamond as their king and crowned him in the year of the Incarnation of Our Lord Jesus Christ 418, when Theodosius was Emperor of Rome. It happened that Theodosius had a nephew, a very handsome knight, strong, valiant and capable of any feat that would test his honour. This knight ruled the land of Pannonia, which today is called Hungary, and his name was Reinbert. One night he dreamt that he was hunting a golden lion and it seemed to him that he was capturing it. In the morning, when he was awakened ...]

Reinbert's fictio, its novelistic identity, is marked, as a narrative threshold, by the first action that the character performs: *cil Reinbers songa une nuit* ..., 'one night Reinbert dreamt ...'; whereas everything that appears before this threshold is presented as a historical (pseudo-)chronology – a calendar, an annalistic computation – with the purpose of 'dating' the *fictio* of the novel. This relationship between the fictional *inside* and the *outside* of History is then made explicit by means of the same device already used in *Cristal et Clarie*. That is, in *Reinbert*, too, the novel begins in an *outside*, through a link with its book-form. In fact, that chronology, that 'historiographical page' which precedes the hero's dream, comes from another text also already existing in the Arsenal manuscript. This time it is a *Chronique* of the kings of France that, a few pages earlier (297r), begins and continues with exactly the same words as the novel: *Segnor et dames, el commencement des regnes, quant nom furent mis es terres* ...[59] Thus, the reader rereads once again within the novel a 'real book' that he had already read – in the same manuscript – 'outside the novel'. In this case, the introjection of the 'historical book' in the novel text clearly performs a function of narrative coordination between the historical multiplicity of the 'narratable' and the novelistic singularity of the event. Rewriting the 'historiographical book' as the incipit of the novel actually means introducing into the fiction a 'material proof' – that is, a book already read – that the narrative is included in reality. As in de Musset's *Confession*, the historiographical discourse becomes the threshold for entering the novel.

In the case of both *Cristal et Clarie* and *Reinbert*, this kind of textual phenomenon is amplified by the fact that these exchanges between the novel and its manuscript context take place within the boundaries of the same book – within the miscellaneous form, in the *varietas*, of the manuscript Arsenal 3516. Thus, the reader of this codex will witness, on the one hand, the falsification of the 'courtly book' inside the 'book of *Cristal et Clarie*' and, on the other, the prolongation of a historiographical chronicle into a chivalric novel. In both cases, the *outside* is pulled 'inside the novel' not so much as a real referent – that is, as mere courtly ideology or as a concrete sequence of historical facts – but rather through the image of the corresponding books – the 'book of courtly doctrine' and the 'historiographical book'. By reducing its exterior and real referents – its *outside* – to the status of mere book-objects, the novel ends up overturning the relation: it is the 'novelistic book' that can claim the greatest degree of reality, since only the novel is able to falsify – or reduce to *fictio* – all books other than its own.

Notes

1 Foerster 1888, 1 (20–21).
2 Furetière, *Roman bourgeois*, 198. Equally embarrassing requests are expressed by General Stumm von Bordwehr – a parody of those who fail to fit in with the intellectual elite – in Musil's *The Man without Qualities*.
3 Ibid.
4 Ibid., 201.
5 Stendhal *Lamiel*, 67.
6 *Long à écrire* – 'yet to be written', 'far from being written' – although the book is already in the hands of its readers. See Barthes 2015, 36: "la seule chose qui raconte la *Recherche du temps perdu*, c'est le Vouloir-Écrire. […]. Résumer la *Recherche*, c'est l'histoire du Vouloir-Écrire, sinon ça n'est pas résumable".
7 On 'novelistic nostalgia', see Fuksas 2020.
8 Thibaudet 2000, 38.
9 On the book-form in the study of textual traditions, see Antonelli 1985, 207–211 and Busby 2002.
10 Azzam, Collet, Foehr-Janssens 2007.
11 On miscellaneous traditions, see Petrucci 1986, 2004 and Martina 2020.
12 See Walters 1985.
13 See above, the first chapter.
14 On the debate around miscellaneous manuscripts and Romance literature, see Trachsler 2019.
15 Lanata 2020, 10–12.
16 Ibid., 140.
17 In contemporary criticism, 'outside the text' or 'inside the text' obviously recalls the categories discussed by Genette (1987). The French critic used such expressions to identify the paratexts (titles, prefaces, dedications and so on) that allow entry and transit in the text. To avoid misunderstanding, here and in the following pages these two expressions will be used in a simpler way: they serve only to express the linguistic articulation between the reality outside the text – the world – and its representation within the same text.

18 "L'infini du monde représentable", Del Lungo 2003, 24.
19 Butor (2019, 130–157) related the 'simultaneity of narrative events' to the book-form, that is, the horizontality of *mise en page* and reading.
20 Auerbach 1953, 549.
21 Balzac, *Albert Savarus*; italics added.
22 He was apparently Charles Weiss, see Pellini 2017, 192, n. 167.
23 See Genette 1972, 240: "ce personnage n'en serait pas moins diégétique, quoique réel – tout comme Richelieu chez Dumas [...] ou la princesse Mathilde chez Proust. Bref, on ne confondra pas le caractère extradiégétique avec l'existence historique réelle".
24 Ibid., 244.
25 Critics have often highlighted this level of significance; see Boiron, Payen 1970; Haidu 1972; de Looze 1990; Virdis 2001.
26 Renaut de Beaujeu, *Le bel inconnu*, 190–191.
27 James 1884, 504.
28 Ibid., 515; italics added.
29 See Haidu 1972, 48–49 and his bibliographical discussion; italics added.
30 "vos feroit Guinglain retrover / s' amie, que il a perdue".
31 In the comparison with the 'narrating voice', it is important to note this phatic function, claimed by the *pucelle*: *je sui cele / qui fis savoir...* ('it is I who have made known...'), *Et si sui cele ... la vois que vos aprés oïstes* ('I am the voice you have heard').
32 Let us say in passing that, as was already the case in Chrétien's *Erec*, adventure and marriage – narrative possibility and conjugal choice – become in the *Bel inconnu* the dialectical poles within which textual *fictio* can exist; marriage would thus mark the re-entry into the reality of the *outside*, the exit threshold from the book to life.
33 Blanchot 2000, 15–16.
34 Ibid., 330.
35 See Fuksas 2020.
36 Barthes 2015, 36.
37 Genette 1972, 246–251.
38 Köhler 1990.
39 "à *quelle occasion* je fus pris d'abord de la maladie du siècle", de Musset, *La confession d'un enfant du siècle*.
40 Balzac, *La Duchesse de Langeais*, 87. It is well known that in Balzac's work the category of *hasard* is almost an equivalent of the narrative structure. Moreover, Balzac often conceals 'diegetic randomness' through its opposite, that is, the 'secret plot', the 'Conspiracy': "la main qui soutenait ce garçon dans la vie n'avait plus fait sentir son pouvoir que dans une seule circonstance", Balzac, *Les employés*, 36 – on conspiracy in Balzac's novels see Marceau 1970, 381–394; Sugden 2021.
41 Köhler 1990, 7.
42 Ibid., 13.

43 Roland Barthes also raised a similar question: "pourquoi *cette* histoire-là parmi tant d'autres? [...] Pourquoi cette histoire plutôt qu'une autre? Pour moi, le grand critère pour reconnaitre une *œuvre* [...] ce serait qu'elle dégage un sentiment de *nécessité*", Barthes 2015, 49.
44 *L'estoire*, vol. 1, § 6–8; italics added.
45 See Séguy 2015.
46 For Nerval's oneiric writing and its consequences on diegesis, see Illouz 1997, 182: "la focalisation du récit de rêves tend ainsi à mettre en abyme la relation du narrateur au narrataire dans la relation du narrateur au personnage".
47 Nerval, *Sylvie*, 137; italics added.
48 Proust himself noted this limitation in Nerval's writing: his 'narrating self', which relates stages of semi-oneiric vision (as in *Sylvie* and other tales), can exist discursively "jusqu'au moment où le sommeil rend le dédoublement impossible" (Proust, *Contre Sainte-Beuve*, 150). In fact, by falling asleep, Nerval's self cannot be, at the same time, diegetic agent and narrator, and therefore in his writing we observe a break of time between the dreamer and the writer.
49 The relations between 'narrative actualisation' and 'diegetic possibilities' are investigated by the so-called theory of possible texts; see the studies collected in Escola 2012.
50 White 2014, 147.
51 Barthes 2015, 49; see also Fuksas 2020.
52 The codex has been studied by Guggenbühl (1998), see also Gingras 2017, 411–457.
53 "Qui ces vers voldra retenir / et bien entendre et bien oïr, / oïr i pora qu'est amors" (vv. 3–5), 'Anyone who will pay attention to those verses, and well understand and listen them, will hear what love is', Breuer 1915.
54 See Toniutti 2017.
55 Actually, the entire text of *Cristal et Clarie* is made up of quotations taken from previous courtly narratives.
56 "les quisses li a cil overtes", 'he opened her thighs' (v. 8368).
57 See Toniutti 2017, 342–343.
58 Woledge 1939.
59 Ibid., 90.

References

R. Antonelli, "Interpretazione e critica del testo", in *Letteratura italiana*, ed. A. Asor Rosa, IV, *L'interpretazione*, Torino, Einaudi, 1985, pp. 141–243.

E. Auerbach, *Mimesis. The Representation of Reality in Western Literature*, Princeton, Princeton University Press, 1953 [or. ed. E.

Auerbach, *Mimesis. Dargestellte Wirklichkeit in der abendländischen Literatur*, Bern, Franke, 1946].

W. Azzam, O. Collet, Y. Foehr-Janssens, "Cohérence et éclatement: réflexion sur les recueils littéraires du Moyen Âge", *Babel*, 16 (2007), pp. 31–59.

H. de Balzac, *Albert Savarus*, ed. J. Milhit, Paris, Livre de poche, 2015.

H. de Balzac, *La Duchesse de Langeais – La Fille aux yeux d'or*, ed. R. Fortassier, Paris, Gallimard, 1976.

H. de Balzac, *Les employés*, ed. A.M. Meininger, Paris, Gallimard, 1985.

R. Barthes, *La préparation du roman. Cours au Collège de France (1978–1979 et 1979–1980)*, Paris, Seuil, 2015.

M. Blanchot, "La rencontre de l'imaginaire", in Id., *Le livre à venir*, Paris, Gallimard, 2016 [or. ed. Paris, Gallimard, 1959].

F. Boiron, J.C. Payen, "Structure et sens du *Bel inconnu* de Renaut de Beaujeu", *Le Moyen Âge*, 76 (1970), pp. 15–26.

H. Breuer (ed.), *Cristal und Clarie, altfranzösischer Abenteuerroman des XIII. Jahrhunderts*, Dresden, Gesellschaft für romanische Literatur, 1915.

K. Busby, *Codex and Context. Reading Old French Verse Narrative in Manuscript*, 2 vols., Amsterdam and New York, Rodopi, 2002.

M. Butor, "Le livre comme objet", in Id., *Essais sur le roman*, Paris, Gallimard, 2019, pp. 130–157 [or. ed. Paris, Éditions de Minuit, 1964].

R. de Beaujeu, *Le bel inconnu*, ed. G. Perrie Williams, Paris, Champion, 1983.

L. de Looze, "Generic clash, reader response, and the poetics of the non-ending in *Le bel inconnu*", in *Courtly Literature: Culture and Context. Selected Papers from the 5th Triennial Congress of the International Courtly Literature Society* (Dalfsen, 9–16 August 1986), ed. K. Busby, E. Kooper, Amsterdam and Philadelphia, Benjamins, 1990, pp. 113–112.

A. de Musset, *La confession d'un enfant du siècle*, ed. S. Ledda, Paris, Flammarion, 2010.

A. Del Lungo, *L'incipit romanesque*, Paris, Seuil, 2003.

M. Escola (ed.), *Théorie des textes possibles*, Amsterdam, Rodopi, 2012.

Y. Foehr-Janssens, O. Collet (eds.), *Le recueil au Moyen Âge. Le Moyen Âge central*, Turnhout, Brepols, 2010.

W. Foerster (ed.), *Cligés von Christian von Troyes*, Halle, Max Niemeyer, 1888.

A.P. Fuksas, "Storia, mito e rispecchiamento esemplare nel romanzo medievale in versi", *Le Forme e la Storia*, 13 (2020), pp. 105–128.

A.P. Fuksas, "Il romanzo come Forma Patetica della Nostalgia", in *Un'invenzione romanza: il romanzo e le sue trasformazioni nelle letterature medievali e moderne*, Atti del VI seminario internazionale di studio (L'Aquila, 26–27 Novembre 2019), ed. L. Spetia [= *Spolia*, 2020], pp. 151–166.

A. Furetière, *Le roman bourgeois*, ed. M. Roy-Garibal, Paris, Flammarion, 2001.
G. Genette, *Figures III*, Paris, Seuil, 1972.
G. Genette, *Seuils*, Paris, Seuil, 1987.
F. Gingras, "Roman et livre", in Id., *Le Bâtard conquérant. Essor et expansion du genre romanesque au Moyen Âge*, Paris, Champion, 2017.
C. Guggenbühl, *Recherches sur la composition et la structure du ms. Arsenal 3516*, Basel and Tübingen, Francke Verlag, 1998.
P. Haidu, "Realism, Convention, Fictionality and the Theory of Genres in *Le bel inconnu*", *L'Esprit Créateur*, 12 (1972), pp. 37–60.
J.N. Illouz, *Nerval, le 'rêveur en prose'. Imaginaire et écriture*, Paris, PUF, 1997.
H. James, "The Art of Fiction", *Longman's Magazine*, 4 (1884), pp. 502–521.
E. Köhler, *Il romanzo e il caso. Da Stendhal a Camus*, Bologna, Il Mulino, 1990 [or. ed. E. Köhler *Der literarische Zufall. Das Mögliche und die Notwendigkeit*, München, Fink, 1973].
G. Lanata, *Poetica pre-platonica. Testimonianze e frammenti*, Roma, Edizioni di Storia e Letteratura, 2020 [or. ed. Firenze, La Nuova Italia, 1963].
L'estoire du saint Graal, ed. J.P. Ponceau, Paris, Champion, 1997.
F. Marceau, *Balzac et son monde*, Paris, Gallimard, 1970.
P.A. Martina, *Il romanzo francese in versi e la sua produzione manoscritta*, Strasbourg, Éditions de linguistique et de philologie, 2020.
G. de Nerval, *Les filles du feu–Les chimères*, ed. L. Cellier, Paris, Flammarion, 1965.
P. Pellini (ed.), *Albert Savarus*, by H. de Balzac, Palermo, Sellerio, 2017.
A. Petrucci, "Dal libro unitario al libro miscellaneo", in *Tradizione dei classici. Trasformazione della cultura*, ed. A. Giardina, Roma-Bari, Laterza, 1986, pp. 173–187.
A. Petrucci, "Introduzione", in *Il codice miscellaneo. Tipologie e funzioni. Atti del convegno internazionale (Cassino, 14–17 Maggio 2003)*, ed. E. Crisci, O. Pecere [= *Segno e Testo*, 2 (2004)], pp. 3–16.
M. Proust, *Contre Sainte-Beuve*, ed. B. de Fallois, Paris, Gallimard 2019 [or. ed. Paris, Gallimard, 1954].
M. Séguy, "Le livre dans le récit", *Cahiers de recherches médiévales et humanistes*, 29 (2015), pp. 111–128.
Stendhal, *Lamiel*, ed. A.M. Meininger, Paris, Gallimard, 1983.
R. Sugden, "Vers une poétique de la conspiration chez Balzac", in *Actes de l'Atelier de la SERD*, 'L'Imaginaire des sociétés secrètes dans la littérature du XIXe siècle', 2021.
A. Thibaudet, *Il lettore di romanzi*, Napoli, Liguori, 2000 [or. ed. A. Thibaudet, *Le liseur de romans*, Paris, Crès, 1925].

G. Toniutti, "Mise en recueil et assemblage des contraires. 'Cristal et Clarie', 'D'Amour' et le manuscrit Arsenal 3516", *Le Moyen Âge*, 123 (2017), pp. 339–349.

R. Trachsler, "De l'objet au texte et vice versa. Le statut du recueil manuscrit dans les études de la littérature du Moyen Âge", in *Le Moyen Âge dans le texte*, ed. B. Grévin, A. Mairey, Paris, Editions de la Sorbonne, 2019, pp. 45–58.

M. Virdis, *Lezione sul Bel inconnu*, Lecture at University of Cagliari, 11 June 2001, available online: https://presnaghe.wordpress.com/2010/03/22/lezione-sul-bel-inconnu/.

L. Walters, "Le rôle du scribe dans l'organisation des manuscrits de Chrétien de Troyes", *Romania*, 106 (1985), pp. 303–325.

H. White, *Metahistory*, Baltimore, John Hopkins University Press, 2014 [or. ed. Baltimore, John Hopkins University Press, 1973].

B. Woledge, "'Reinbert': a neglected French Romance of the Thirteenth Century", *Medium Aevum*, 8 (1939), pp. 85–117, pp. 173–192.

3 Dreaming the incipit (towards Proust and the *Rose*)

1 Plotted times

In *Cristal et Clarie* and *Reinbert*, the fictional text from the very beginning establishes its own relationship with the external world. In both cases, the incipit of the story incorporates within the work a pre-existing book that was already real and existing in the 'out-of-text'. That book, introjected into the novel from the beginning, performs a transit function between the reader's world and the fictional universe.

Broadly speaking, the position of such 'inventions' in the incipit often involves the overall structure of the text. Indeed, every incipit always involves an arbitrary choice:[1] by beginning the diegesis, the narrator will have to extract a section of 'life' from the representable whole, in order to choose a starting point, including the fictional events within the artefactual limits of the incipit. In other words, while single moments or existential events give an impression of continuity – of non-divisibility – in life ('outside the text'), in its linguistic and narrative representation reality appears resected, always circumscribed between two thresholds – of entry and exit. Thus, for any narrative the incipit is a moment of particular fragility, since by merely beginning, the work must face up to its fictitious nature: having to begin is in fact an admission of non-existence. The narrative incipit must therefore find a way to take charge of this problem, in order to resolve "la relation – de continuité ou de contigüité – entre l'intérieur et l'extérieur".[2]

Once again, let us take an example from two incipit in Balzac. Both produce a space of 'chronological reference', or 'contextual

DOI: 10.4324/9781003223641-3

Dreaming the incipit 69

relevance', in their respective novels – that is, an incipit related to the *outside*.

À l'époque où commence cette histoire la presse de Stanhope et les rouleaux à distribuer l'encre ne fonctionnait pas encore dans les petites imprimeries de province [...]. Ce Séchard était un ancien compagnon pressier.

(*Illusions perdues*[3])

[This story begins at the time when the Stanhope and ink distribution rollers were not yet used in small printing shops of the provinces [...]. Séchard was a long-time press worker].

À Paris, où les hommes d'étude et de pensée ont quelques analogies en vivant dans le même milieu, vous avez dû rencontrer plusieurs figures semblables à celle de M. Rabourdin, que ce récit prend au moment où il est chef de bureau [...]. À l'époque ou le prend cette Étude, vous eussiez remarqué chez lui l'air froidement résigné.

(*Les Employés*[4])

[In Paris, where men of study and thought bear a certain likeness to one another, living in the same milieu, you must have met with several resembling Mr. Rabourdin, whom this story portrays at the moment when he was head of bureau [...]. At the epoch this Study portrays him, you would have noticed in him the coldly resigned air].

The *Illusions perdues*, the novel of a pretentious young man born into a family of provincial printers, begins *à l'époque...*, that is, in a time that is not exclusively fictional, but instead available to common historical experience. *À l'époque* serves to 'date' the fictional narrative in History; it is a boundary time, which belongs as much *outside* as *inside* the novel. The extra-textual referents of this chronology consist of certain objects: the press machines. From a pragmatic perspective, printing rollers and Stanhope's press are nothing more than a date; they serve to signify not so much themselves, as the reality or the epoch in which those objects were used – or rather, were not yet used 'in the small provincial printing shops': the *terminus ante quem* for the novel's incipit. Those objects are the 'concrete detail',[5] that is, the semi-casual *outside*, which, placed in the incipit, simulates an analogy with the historical time. In *Les Employés*, in contrast, the relation between the fictional interiority and the exteriority of History is developed, at the incipit of the story, as a relationship between reality and a *casus fictus*, a 'hypothetical case'. If we had known the clerks of bureaucratic and administrative Paris, then we would have seen several men resembling Monsieur Rabourdin, that is, the 'fictitious person' whose appearance in the text opens up the fictional time proper, as opposed to the historical or sociological time included in the deixis *à Paris ... à l'époque*. Therefore, the incipit of *Les Employés* generates the novel as if the latter were a hypothesis on reality. This 'conditional structure' is grammatically summarised in the clause *vous eussiez remarqué*, 'you would have noticed ...'. It is a linguistic sign, that is, the verbal threshold that establishes the novel as a hypothetical emanation[6] of an *outside* – as the projection of all those 'real' clerks resembling Monsieur Rabourdin's *casus fictus*.

The purpose of these narrative solutions is to coordinate two different temporalities: on the one hand, the external time, which is the common time, recursively perceived 'out of the novel' – a time available to the reader's common experience – and on the other hand, the singular time of the novelistic events – a time that realises inside the *fictio* what the 'out of the fiction' contains in the form of the possible. The relation between these two temporalities – which are part of any realistic incipit – operates on the grammar of the entire narrative.

Genette's distinctions concerning 'narrative frequency' are useful in this regard. I refer specifically to the pages in which the critic distinguished two kinds of novelistic temporality: the so-called singular narrative scenes (or *singualtives*) and the iterative scenes, as two opposite diegetic trends. The former are narrative sequences in which the text tells of an event that occurs once in the diegesis; the latter are those sequences in which an event that occurs several times in the diegesis is narrated once – as in the iterative formulae 'every day he went ...', 'sometimes he said ...'.[7] If we implement this distinction for the incipit in these two works by Balzac, we observe how the evocation of the *outside* implies an iterative relation. The print rollers and the Stanhope are verbalised as if they were a recursive feature of the external reality, to the point of representing an entire epoch – given their iterative nature. The Parisian clerks, the 'real' ones resembling Rabourdin, are presented to the reader's observation – the 'you' of the incipit – as if the latter could iteratively meet some of them every day. From those examples, one can deduce a technique of the novel – at least in its 'classical realism' phase: the qualification of external reality in 'repetitive' or 'serial' terms with respect to the singularity of the narrative action. Moreover, this 'repetitiveness' of the *outside* is not limited to iteration in time – the typographical machines as the duration of an epoch – but can also concern the perceptive iteration, that is, the fact that a certain element of reality can be observed several times – or to put another way, *quelques analogies* between the Parisian bureaucracy's clerks.

In short, interaction and singularity are categories of textual hermeneutics relevant to the study of the novel form as a whole. Their dialectic, that is, the prevalence of one or the other, can determine a structural leap in the history of the literary genre. Indeed, those two narratological notions mirror long-standing critical ideas – albeit from different perspectives. For example, the notions of iteration and singularity seem to reflect Lukács's main dichotomy, which distinguished 'interiority' and 'adventure'[8] as contrasting trends of novelistic language. Apart from the obvious distinctions that developed over time with respect to this opposition,[9] such a dichotomy emphasises certain actual features. For instance, the medieval novel, which enters wholly into the anthropological category of *aventure* – even when its contents are erotic, idyllic or pertain to other sub-genres[10] – allows for the comparison of different hermeneutic notions: those of Lukács and those of narratological analysis, which distinguish iteration and singularity.

In fact, the medieval novel is structurally a 'novel of repetition': the hero normally faces sequentially a series of events with a similar structure. However, the 'repetitiveness' of his adventure[11] has a particular quality: it tends to be non-iterative. That is, the 'similar scenes' are narrated each time they occur, so that each time they are retold individually. In principle, medieval writing does not envisage – and indeed rejects – iterative formulas such as 'for years the knight faced many adventures', 'every day he fought and rode …'. Therefore, the adventures of the medieval hero develop along a series of repeated but diegetically singular actions: departures, duels, quests, new departures, new duels, new quests and so on. The episodes, or modules, of the fictional action are similar to each other, yet they are renarrated each time. This textual structure produces sequences of singular adventures that are narrated *only now – only once* as they happen – and yet apparently are paratactic to each other. The narrative character whom Lukács called a 'non-problematic hero' – that is, with little or no distinction between himself and the world – thus operates in a diegesis entirely aimed at the singularity of actions:

> an uninterrupted series of adventures which he himself has chosen. He throws himself into them because life means nothing more to him than the successful passing of tests. His unquestioning interiority forces him to translate that interiority – which he considers to be the average, everyday nature of the real world – into actions.[12]

In contrast with this first 'figure' of novelistic language, Lukács identified a second kind of hero, one whose "soul is wider and larger than the destinies that life has to offer it",[13] that is, an 'excess character', no longer corresponding to the 'adventures' that are offered to him; a new hero, incomplete on the level of his singular actions. It is a radical shift from the pole of action to that of interiority. The character will then no longer operate along the sequential line of his adventures but in a different subjective time.

Genette, too, used the categories of singularity and iteration to date and periodise some historical phases of the novelistic genre. Namely, he observed how these two 'forms of frequency' – that is, singularity and iteration – follow one another throughout the history of the modern novel. In texts in which the critic still recognised the features of the 'traditional plot', singular sequences would prevail over iterative scenes. According to Genette, the traditional diegesis would arrange the text along a narrative line of 'singular actions'. Even where the traditional plot includes iterative inserts, such as descriptions of spaces or psychological portraits, those sequences would still be "au service du récit 'proprement dit', qui est le récit singulative",[14] that is, that kind of diegesis in which the actions are narrated *once*, as they are the core, the 'event' of the fictional adventure. The opposite movement towards a modern iterative diegesis – which Genette dated to Flaubert's work – obviously entails a rebalancing between the two kinds of frequency, that is, a trend towards increasing the 'recursive' temporality: "non ce qui *s'est passé*, mais ce qui *se passait* [...], régulièrement, rituellement, tous le jours, ou tous les dimanches, ou tous les samedis ...".[15] From this perspective, we can perceive a certain degree of translatability between Lukács's aesthetic categories and Genette's tools of narratological analysis:[16] their two antinomies – 'adventure/interiority' on the one side and 'singularity/iteration' on the other – can overlap. The *aventure* of the medieval novel allows for a hermeneutical exchange between the two critical dichotomies.

Indeed, within the *aventure*'s medieval plot, the object of the narrative *quête* – whether it be the love for Guinevere or the search for the Grail, liberating a captive maiden or winning her hand in marriage – may vary from time to time, from text to text, according to the different characters and the goals of their particular chivalric identity. Nevertheless, the diegetic phases of the *quête*, its internal moments, will always develop according to the 'anticipatory void'[17] of the adventure itself: the hero knows in advance that his personal identity will emerge from an indeterminate repetition of a long sequence of 'singularities' and actions. Thus, the different phases of the adventure occur, separately, from time to time, but at the same time they are usually foreshadowed and foretold by the hero's expectation. Two examples from the work of Chrétien de Troyes can illustrate this function. In the *Erec*, the last sequence of the adventure is pre-announced by the characters of the story, as if its action were perpetually waiting and available to those who wish to perform it. In fact, before the adventure has begun, the characters know its contents: "ce que je sai de l'avanture / qui tant est perilleuse e dure" (vv. 5431–5432), 'what I know about the adventure, which is very dangerous and hard'. Similarly, in the *Chevalier au Lion*, the adventure of the "Fontaine qui bout" is not only pre-narrated by a knight who had already been confronted with it, but is also almost signalled to Yvain along his way, since that adventure too has always – and repeatedly – been available to his hero: "un santier qui la te manra / [...]. / La fontaine verras qui bout" (vv. 375–380),[18] 'a path that will lead you there [...], you will see the bubbling fountain'.

An analysis based on Lukács's categories – that is, active participation in the world *versus* subjective times of interiority – would perhaps fail to understand this specific dialectic between the singularity of the adventures (action) and the time of their expectation (interiority), just as a narratology of iteration – based on Genette's assumptions – would perhaps prefer to look for the 'temporal frequency' in a diegesis projected into the past – *ce qui ce passait*. In contrast, in the medieval novel the relations between singularity and iteration – between the adventure and its expectation – seem rather to produce a diegetic link between *ce qui se passe* and *ce qui se passera*, between present and future – the events in progress and the expectation of the following moment. However, in the medieval narrative, the diegetic future – 'what will happen' – will be an adventure again – that is, again a singular scene. Herein lies a difference between the medieval diegesis and the modern novel: the former tends to re-narrate each time what each time happens again, thus effectively transforming an iterative narrative matter into a sequence of singularities.[19] The possibility that 'nothing more will happen' – that *rien ne se passera* – instead defines a deeper function in the medieval novel, underlying the dialectic between singular and iterative tenses. For instance, the *recreantise* of the *Erec*, that is, the narrative situation in which the hero is no longer able to act, serves this very aim: it is a first shift, in the diachrony of the novelistic genre, towards a relocation of the diegesis in the 'memorial times' of iteration. By foregoing every *chevalerie*, that is, every adventure or diegetic singularity, Chrétien's novelistic couple enters the *longtemps* of erotic-conjugal iteration. For these reasons, in the *Erec* the narrative sequence opening the 'novel of the idle and *recreant* couple' begins with a new and different adverb of time. That is, the central sequence of the Chrétien's novel begins on an iterating locution – 'often' – that immediately denotes the non-adventurousness of the scene, "*sovant* estoit midi passez / einçois que de lez li levast" – 'often it was already past noon before he rose from beside her' (vv. 2446–2447). The adverb – often, *sovant* – displays our entry into a new temporality of iterative actions.

Sometimes, the medieval novel makes explicit the 'delays' and the 'temporal voids' of its diegesis, that is, the risk that the book, without any *aventure*, cannot begin. The *Jaufre*, for example, stages the possibility that the adventures will no longer occur: "nepz – ditz lo rei – , fait enselar / que irem aventura cercar / pueis qu en esta cort non venon", 'nephew – the king said – , put the saddles on and we will seek adventures, since in this court they do not come' (vv. 165–167).[20] The Arthurian prose of the *Lancelot* cycle is even clearer: its fictional narrative can solely conclude through "la fin de cels de cui il avoit fait mencion",[21] 'the end of the characters of whom it had spoken', that is, interrupting – by the death of the characters – the 'time of adventures', which ultimately coincides with diegetic times.

According to this perspective, it would be possible to attempt a genealogy of the 'modern iterative form', following a great shift in the focalisation of narrative scenes from the Middle Ages onwards. The bed of Erec and Enide, in which the impasse between heroism and eroticism is realised, the Arthurian court of *Jaufre*, blocked by the non-happening of the adventures, and dozens of similar scenes in the medieval literary tradition, are narrative situations of 'delay', of waiting or suspension of diegetic singularities. In such scenes the hero has missed the possibility of performing his actions. In short, these narrative situations stage the risk that an empty and repetitive time[22] replaces the singular time of action. For the 'modern novelistic form', such scenes would have offered as many opportunities for iterative narration, virtually to be developed at the level of diegetic functions. Like the Proustian *drame du coucher*, nothing more than *recreantise* or iterative waiting for the maternal goodnight, that is, an empty time in which the novel begins, a time that Marcel would like to prolong – "à ce que se prolongeât le temps de répit [suspended time] où maman n'est pas encore venue".[23] Like, too, the times Emma Bovary spends at the window: "Emma était accoudée à sa fenêtre (elle s'y mettait souvent ...)" (II, VII). Ultimately, from this hypothesis we could deduce that the modern 'novel of iteration' develops as a 'filling' of those diegetic voids in which the medieval narrative, in contrast, perceived the risk of its end: that is, the crisis of singular sequences.

2 The dreaming incipit (towards Proust)

This complex relationship between iteration and singularity – that is, between what the diegesis repeats over time and what it makes happen only once – emerges clearly in the incipit of some novels: for instance, in those texts beginning 'in bed', that is, with the narrative voice in a sleeping/dreaming condition. Obviously, the 'dreaming incipit' is an extremely broad literary situation that performs innumerable and different functions,[24] from the psychological to the meta-textual. Even awakenings – 'the morning of life', as Nerval says – or a state of hallucinatory insomnia can be part of it in various ways. An approach to certain texts in which the 'I in bed' appears in the novel's incipit may, then, circumscribe a new sphere of textual functions.[25] We are ultimately interested in those cases in which the 'incipit in bed' seems to re-present inside the text the largely para-textual problem of duration, of the conjunction between the time of writing and the time of diegesis.

Knut Hamsun's *Hunger* (1890)[26] provides a good example of how this incipit typology can serve the coordination of singularity and iteration:

> It was *during the time I wandered about starved in Christiania*: Christiania, this strange city, from which no man departs without carrying the traces of his sojourn there.
> I was lying awake in my attic and I heard a clock below strike six. It was already broad daylight, and people had begun to go up and down stairs. [...]. The instant I opened my eyes I began, from sheer force of habit, to wonder if I had anything to rejoice over that day. I had been somewhat hard-up lately [...]. A few times I had kept to my bed for the day with vertigo. [...]. It grew lighter and lighter, and I took to reading the advertisements near the door. [...]. I opened the window and looked out [...]. The ever-increasing noise in the streets lured me out. The bare room, the floor of which rocked up and down with every step I took across it, seemed like a gaping sinister coffin. There was no proper fastening to the door either, and no stove. I used to lie on my socks at night to dry them a little by the morning. The only thing I had to divert myself with was a little red rocking-chair [...]. I stood up and searched through a bundle.
>
> (italics added)

The first sentence of the novel sets out in strongly iterative terms ("during the time ...") the event that will recur throughout the work, the protagonist's hunger, while the singularity, that is, the one-time event in the diegesis, appears immediately after: in the 'incipit in bed', with the character barely awake – "I was lying awake ...". Given these two narrative points, the development of that opening piece is a back and forth between iteration and singularity. On the one hand, we can observe events narrated as if they were only now occurring in the text – "I began ... to wonder", "I took to reading", "I opened the window" ... – and, on the other hand, events that are clearly iterative – "I had been somewhat hard-up lately", "a few times I had kept to my bed". Moreover, within such a diegetic arrangement a sequence emerges that is apparently descriptive, but actually increases the degree of iteration: this is the passage about the squalor of the attic ("the bare room ..."), that is, the recurrent perception of a space, which does not concern the 'singular awakening' placed in the novel's incipit, but instead should have occurred identically every morning. The fact that the descriptive sequence is substantially an iterative piece is also evident by virtue of the narrator's sudden return to bed, which is actually a temporal regression, that is, a return to an indefinite series of previous awakenings, in which the attic had already appeared in its squalor. In fact, a few lines earlier, the 'I' had got up to look out of the window ("I opened the window and looked out") – and thus a 'singular event' had occurred; by contrast, the short sequence on the squalor of the room ends with an explicit iteration: "*I used* to lie on my socks at night ...". This 'usual and repetitive' action leads the character back to his bed, recursively in time, in a series of previous awakenings. The diegetic time in which the 'I' goes to the window and the time in which the room displays its squalor – completed by the time in which the 'I' used to lie on his socks – are not the same chronology. Although they align in the diegesis, the first one is a singular time, while the others are clearly iterative and recursive. Finally, the beginning of an increasingly 'singularised' diegesis, that is, the start of the 'unique facts' of the 'fictional adventure', is marked by the last sentence – "I stood up and searched ..." – in which the 'I' gets out of bed and breaks the cyclical succession of singularity and iteration.

Let us take a second example from Hugo von Hofmannsthal's *Andreas* (1932),[27] although it is not really an incipit but rather a re-beginning:

> He was ashamed in his own sight and did not want to think of the three disastrous days in Carinthia, but the face of the rascally servant already stood before him and, whether he would or not, he had to recall it all minutely [...]: *every day, morning or evening*, it would all came back to him.

78 *Dreaming the incipit*

> *Once more* he was in the inn 'Zum Schwert' in Villach after a hard day.
>
> (italics added)

Andreas, the novelistic hero, is in Venice, but at an earlier point he had travelled through Carinthia; this journey keeps coming back to him. Thus, in the passage from Hofmannsthal the act of remembering is represented in iterative terms – "every day" – as a recurring event, placed alongside a series of moments in which the hero probably wakes up or goes to bed – "morning or evening". By contrast, the singular event, that is, the unique fact in the diegesis, is the content of that iterative recollection: "Once more he was in the inn ...", back again in Carinthia. It is therefore, in Hofmannsthal's case, a simple analepsis. The narrator must inform us of what happened before, and the morning or evening iteration of the memory performs the function of a 'summary scene' of the past – 'once more ...'. The character came back to a previous diegetic time; iteration and singularity follow one another. The reader who leaves Andreas in a Venetian house, occupied by his iteration, by the repetition of the memory – confident that he will find him in the same place when the memory of it is over – also enters into the singularity of the remembered events. The assurance offered beforehand to the reader that the events in progress are repetitive – and therefore in Venice, at that moment, nothing 'singular' is happening – opens the text to the analeptical time of what happened only once in the Austrian inn.

Compared to Hamsun's incipit, the passage in Hofmannsthal's *Andreas* is a simple 'narrative frame': the memory of the journey to Carinthia is embedded in the same Venetian setting; it is a re-beginning, framed in the iterative memory that 'every morning' or 'every evening' re-happens. The result is that the 'diegetic before' – the journey to Carinthia – is quite distinct from the iteration of the 'Venetian present', during which the 'before' is remembered. In contrast, in Hamsun's novel iteration and singularity coexist on the same plane: that 'singular' morning in which the narrating-I wakes up – and in which the novel begins – repeats the same events that have already occurred in a series of similar awakenings. The incipit's position excludes the analepsis: the diegesis has just begun, there is nothing to recapitulate, and thus the iteration seems to overflow, anteriorly, into the 'out-of-text'. In short,

Hamsun's awakening recursively occurs, and the reader cannot distinguish that specific morning from others that we imagine have already happened. This is possible because in *Hunger* the singular scene includes its iterations: the awakening of that single morning repeats the events of every other awakening; namely, what happens *that time* continues to repeat what has happened *each time*. Conversely, in Hofmannsthal the iterative event includes the singular scene: that is, Andreas remembers *each time* what happened *only once*. Therefore, comparing the two passages, Hamsun's incipit establishes a recursive 'habitual time', and thus every morning can coincide with the incipit's time.

From Balzac's Stanhope, which places the fictional happening in the 'duration' of the historical *outside*, to Hamsun's awakening, whose recursive time places the incipit event between the *outside* of previous mornings and the *inside* of 'that morning', the iterative trend has increased somewhat. However, even in Hamsun, the textual plane on which the awakening iteratively occurs is always the diegetic plane; if the scene seems to overflow into 'the novel's before', this is by virtue of its position as the incipit, beyond which the story is instinctively perceived as still non-existent. And thus what happens in the incipit in iterative terms seems to be an event that happened 'from-before-the novel'. But, of course, this is fiction's illusionism, through which the novel's iterative incipit narrativises its own border with exteriority.

Proust is a more difficult and complex case. He is clearly the most prominent and famous example of an 'incipit in bed': "Longtemps, je me suis couché de bonne heure".

Thanks to the publication of Proust's drafts and *cahiers*, from the 1970s onwards, critics have been able to highlight how this first sentence of the novel contains the generative formula of the *Recherche*, that is, the narrative principle that triggers the entire novelistic apparatus. After all, another writer, Georges Perec, already expressed this same critical intuition through a parodic rewriting of the *Recherche*'s incipit: "longtemps je me suis couché par écrit",[28] literally 'for a long time I lay down in writing'.

> We generally utilize the page in the larger of its two dimensions. The same goes for the bed. The bed (or, if you prefer, the page) is a rectangular space, longer than it is wide, in which, or on which, we normally lie longways.[29]

'Lying in bed' and 'laying the writing down on the page' – both actions developed over a 'long time' – is a play on words, a combinatorial equation, in the manner of Perec, that identifies in Proust's novel a fundamental narrative set-up. Perec especially senses the structural link between the time of the incipit event – its absolute iterative quality (*longtemps*) – and the equally 'long time' of the writing, that is, the structural relationship between the bed and the work: they develop a metonymic relationship.

In the overall architecture of the *Recherche*, the novel's incipit is in fact the essential prerequisite for the multiplication of narrative instances, that is, for the textual genesis of the different 'I' that will take voice throughout the storyline.

Longtemps, je me suis couché de bonne heure. Parfois, à peine ma bougie éteinte, mes yeux se fermaient si vite que je n'avais pas le temps de me dire : 'Je m'endors'. Et, une demi-heure après, la pensée qu'il était temps de chercher le sommeil m'éveillait ...

[For a long time I would go to bed early. Sometimes, the candle barely out, my eyes closed so quickly that I did not have time to tell myself: 'I'm falling asleep'. And half an hour later the thought that it was time to try to sleep would awaken me ...]

Once again, Barthes perceived the deep function of this incipit in the grammar of the novel.[30] Indeed, with the opening move alone – in the space of just a few sentences – Proust has provided himself with at least three different narrative instances, which from time to time can develop their own diegetic level: (1) the I who, in an imprecise and recurring past, goes to bed early; (2) the I who, apparently within the iterative times of that past, experiences its insomnia and its 'memorial' awakenings; (3) the I who pronounces the entire incipit, placed in a time x of which we do not know much at the moment and that only at the end of the novel will we guess coincides with the time of the 'I' who awaits the work [*long à écrire* (novel) = *longtemps* (incipit in bed)]. This last 'I' is clearly another narrative instance, compared to the previous voices.

Thereby, the resulting textual structure, like a geometric fractal, is reproduced at subsequent levels of the diegesis. For instance, when the narrator, during the time of his nocturnal awakenings, begins to recall other previous awakenings, the diegetic plane repeats, in fact, the theme already set out in the incipit. It is the *temps de répit*, the time of suspension, or the intermittences between sleep and insomnia, of which waiting for a mother's goodnight, at the beginning of *Swann*, is the first and clearest expression. An 'I' who went to bed early ends up describing an 'I' who could not sleep, while an 'I' waited to fall asleep with *maman*'s goodnight kiss. "The result of this dialectic is that it is vain to wonder if the book's Narrator is Proust (in the civic meaning of the patronymic): it is simply *another* Proust".[31] This narrative ambiguity rests entirely on the 'incipit in bed', since, as Barthes observes, "to say 'I am asleep' is in effect, literally, as impossible as to say 'I'm dead'; writing is precisely that activity which tampers with language – the impossibilities of language – for the advantage of discourse".[32] The 'grammatical outrage' of the novel's first sentence – to enunciate one's sleep[33] – is then resolved through the discursive simultaneity of several voices, which, arranged on coexisting temporalities, can speak about each other. It is in this way that in the *Recherche* there appears the 'character-instance' that critics call the *dormeur éveillé*, the 'awake sleeper', that is, the narrative cluster of the different fictional voices.[34]

It is now an established fact that Proust, from 1908 to 1909, aimed at the definition of a text-form that would be able to express his original intuition, that is, the 'incipit in bed' multiplying the 'I' and the narrating voices. Moreover, it is also now an established fact that only in the 1911 typescript did Proust discover his memorable solution – later printed in the book:[35] *longtemps, je me suis couché* ... The *Cahiers* in which the novelist, before the *Recherche*, attempted to write the *Contre Sainte-Beuve*, an essay of poetics, gradually included in the narrative framework of a morning conversation with his mother, shows the surprising transition from the essay structure to the novel structure: from the never-concluded *Sainte-Beuve* to the *Recherche*. Although it was a long and complex process, the transition from the essay to the novel reveals impressive elements of continuity in the gradual discovery of the deepest forms of narrative.

Looking at that time for an incipit for the narrative framework of his *Sainte-Beuve*, Proust wrote in his *Cahier 1*:[36]

> Au temps de cette matinée dont je veux fixer je ne sais pas pourquoi le souvenir, j'étais déjà malade, j'*étais* je *restais* levé toute la nuit, *et ne dormais* me couchais le matin et dormais le

jour. *Mais le temps n'était pas encore très* Mais alors était encore très près de moi un temps que j'espérais voir revenir et qui aujourd'hui me semble avoir été vécu par une autre personne où j'entrais dans mon lit à dix heures du soir, et avec quelques courts réveils dormais jusqu'au lendemain matin. *Quelquefois* Souvent, à peine ma lampe éteinte, je m'endormais si vite que je n'avais pas le temps de *penser* me dire que je m'endormais. Aussi *quand je me réveillais une heure après* (...) *je ne savais pas que j'avais dormi, je me croyais encore en train de lire le journal* (...); je voulais jeter le journal que je croyais avoir encore en mains, *en me disant* je me disais, il est temps (...) de chercher le sommeil ...

In these sketches, an 'I' states that for some time now he has been ill and goes to bed in the morning, remaining awake at night. Moreover, within this temporality, within the *déjà* of a past that is still going on, this 'I' hoped for the return of a more distant past – a little further away (*était encore très près de moi un temps...*) – in which, instead, he normally went to bed at ten o'clock at night. This further past, compared to the condition of the 'I' who now only sleeps during the morning, is actually a 'diegetic future' – a time to come, which the narrator hopes will (re)happen again, *un temps que j'espérais voir revenir*. The fact that this future has not yet been realised – and thus effectively remains a future, an expectation – is then confirmed by the main sentence: "au temps de cette matinée dont je veux fixer je ne sais pas pourquoi le souvenir, j'étais *déjà* malade ...". Here, the first voice, that is, the one who 'fixes the memory', tells us that at that time 'he was *already* ill', that is, he could no longer sleep at night; and thus syntactically states that he is *still* ill, he *still* sleeps during the day and wakes up at night. Therefore, the past in which a healthy 'I' went to bed at ten o'clock at night coincides with the future expected not only by the ill 'I', but also by the narrator who begins the recollection.

This fragmentation of narrative instances – that is, the arrangement of different diegetic voices – develops from the very beginning in terms of an 'incipit in bed'. Likewise, the always-'in bed' Proust, in the pages of his *Cahiers*, attempted an opposite narrative movement. If, on the one hand, he provided himself with a multiplicity of subjects, on the other hand, he attempted to confuse them, pushing all the different narrative voices towards a single 'time of the text', within which the different 'selves' were aligned in an impossible chronology. Indeed, there is, in the *Cahiers* (and later in the *Recherche*), a narrative image that joins in a single time the ill 'I' who sleeps during the day (1), the healthy 'I' who went to bed at ten o'clock (2), and the 'I' who hopes to sleep again at night (3). It is the image of the 'white line', namely the line of light that is drawn beyond the perimeter of the window – "audessus des rideaux de ma fenêtre cette ligne blanche ...".[37]

> J'étais couché depuis une heure environ. Le jour n'avait pas encore tracé *audessus des rideaux de ma fenêtre cette ligne blanche qui dans l'obscurité de la chambre* dans la chambre là à l'endroit où nous imaginons la commode, cette ligne audessous de laquelle court *se placer* s'installer la fenêtre (...). Parfois c'est une clarté (...) qui nous a trompé et que nous croyons déjà le jour audessus des rideaux de la fenêtre, moins triste que la raie de lumière qui, *sous la porte* dans la chambre d'un hôtel inconnu, trompe le malade; dressé sur son lit par une crise cruelle qui l'a réveillé, il voit cette lumière sous la porte et se dit c'est le jour (...). Bientôt la lumière sous la porte s'éteint et il retombe <tout rentre> dans l'obscurité. Il comprend, sa crise l'avait éveillé presque au moment où il venait de s'endormir. Il est minuit ...

This glimmering line (*Cahier 3*), beyond the curtains or under the door, is thus an image perceived by all the previously disjointed subjects; paradoxically, they are all summoned into the time of the *ligne blanche*. (1) A first 'I' who only goes to sleep in the morning knows that he will soon see that *ligne* – shortly after getting into bed (*le jour n'avait pas encore tracé cette ligne* ...). (2) A second subject, introduced by an unexpected comparison,[38] has instead gone to sleep in the evening, but wakes up, ill, during the night, seeing a faint glow under the door that he mistakes for the sunrise line. (3) This second subject opens up to a third intermediary, to 'the one who has deceived himself' about the nature of that light. Moreover, this latter subject is in fact an emanation of both the first and the second 'I', since both – the sick one who sleeps during the day and the one who wakes up at night – converge in the 'I' who awaits the *ligne blanche*. For the sick one who sleeps in the morning, this *white line* is like an awareness – he knows that the line will appear; for the sick one in the hotel room, the *white line* is a deception; the third one comes out as a 'waiting intermediary' between the previous two subjects.

The two different 'sick subjects' belong to two different times (morning and night), yet they are joined in a single (hyper-)subject, placed in the 'time of the white line' – a borderline time between sleep and awakening for one and the other.[39] This complex strategy, which gradually leads to the formal invention of the *Recherche* and its incipit, thus originates as a "souci de préciser une temporalité paradoxale: coucher à contretemps et anticipation du jour".[40] It is the chronological paradox of going to bed in the morning, when the 'white line' appears, or waking up at night deceiving oneself that morning has arrived with its *ligne blanche*.

In the drafts of the *Cahiers* and *Sainte-Beuve*, the theme of going to bed in a 'reverse temporality' is immediately followed by the image of the morning. It is in fact in the morning that Proust places the episode of *maman*: the scene in which the narrator's mother goes to wish a paradoxical goodnight to the 'I' who only goes to bed in the daytime, bringing with her, along with the morning light, a newly published issue of *Le Figaro* containing an article by her son. The morning conversation on Sainte-Beuve between the narrator and his mother – which constitutes the essayistic core of this first text-form – starts from the reading of that article in *Le Figaro*. Thus, a whole second constructive scenario opens up, which now concerns 'morning time' as a 'time of the work and its realisation': a time of healthy awakening, in daylight, when the work (the *Figaro* article) appears ready to exist. This 'morning time' is in counterpoint to the evening, nocturnal and 'incongruent' times of insomnia, when the work is still searching for itself (*je veux fixer je ne sais pas pourquoi le souvenir ...*) and the novel is fragmented into its different narrative instances. Ultimately, in the *Cahiers*, the mother herself is the 'morning paranymph' of an accomplished work: that article in *Le Figaro*, which the narrator waited for and hoped would become real, during the *longtemps* of his insomnia – "je pensais à un article que j'avais envoyé il y a *longtemps* déjà au Figaro, (...) j'avais espéré chaque matin le trouver dans le journal".[41]

It is therefore no coincidence that in the long transition from the *Cahiers* to the *Recherche*, the 'morning time' – that is, the time of things ready to exist – persists through various text-forms as the time in which the novelistic work reveals itself and appears. The 'morning time' serves in fact to represent the 'miracle' of waking up and finding the book already written next to you. On the one hand, in the *Cahiers* this occurs through the 'auroral episode' of the mother bringing the *Figaro* article. On the other hand, in the *Recherche* it is another morning time, namely the Guermantes *matinée*, that allows the narrator to prepare for his work: "... la nature des circonstances qui m'avaient [...] *au cours de cette matinée* [...] donné à la fois l'idée de *mon œuvre* et la crainte de ne pouvoir la réaliser" (*Temps retrouvé*). Moreover, in the transition from the *Cahiers* to the novel, Proust transforms the mother's morning episode. In the first pages of *Swann*, the mother's non-arrival, her delay in saying goodnight, moves back to evening times – that is, to the times of insomnia, which engender the novel just as a recollection of the mother's delay: "... à ce que se prolongeât *le temps de répit où maman n'est pas encore venue*" (*Du côté de chez Swann*). Between the evening 'incipit in bed' and the 'ending time' of the Guermantes *matinée*, Proust attempted to lengthen the same iterative duration: an intentional 'misunderstanding' about the ongoing hour, within which the moments of lying down and the moments of waking up – although they are distinct in the timeline – represent the same recursive quest for the written work. But actually this 'awaited book', in the diegetic *fictio*, rather than written, is included between the time in which an 'I' wishes to write it – time of insomnia – and the time in which another 'I' is ready to write it – time of the morning.[42]

These narrative arches, joining opposite banks of the diegesis, support the novel's structure. They allow the different diegetic 'I' – as was already the case in the *ligne blanche* of the *Cahiers* – to be co-present in an impossible chronology.

Harold Pinter clearly perceived this principle of Proust's work, and implemented it in his screenplay of the novel,[43] for instance, in the four film sequences in which Pinter connects narrative scenes that the linear diegesis disjoins: (1) the sequence in which "through the drawing room window Mlle Vinteuil and her friend can be seen playing a duet";[44] (2) the sequence in which "through a gap in the hedge" Marcel sees Gilberte for the first time;[45] (3) the scene in which Swann, looking through the window, tries to find out whether Odette is cheating on him;[46] (4) the scene in which Andrée and Albertine prevent Marcel from entering the room, in order to conceal their homoerotic relationship from him.[47] The four sequences scripted by Pinter concern different and irreconcilable times and subjects – and they come from different parts of the novel. However, it is nonetheless evident that the four scenes coexist in a superior synchrony, since they all repeat the same event (the same 'white line'): in this case, the 'same event' is the suspicion that beyond a wall there is a love from which the observer is excluded. The lesbian girls seen beyond the window, as they play a duet, *are the same event* (the same memory) in which Albertine and Andrée conceal, behind the door, their homoerotic friendship from Marcel. The narrator observing Gilberte beyond the hedge *is the same event* (the same memory) as Swann attempting to spy on Odette. These single episodes of the Proustian memory – and others of similar structure – are technically possible thanks to the multiplication of narrative instances, previously established by the 'incipit in bed'.

As has rightly been argued,[48] if Proust had not arranged, from the beginning, the different voices of the narrative – and then overlapped them in the diegesis –, he would have been forced to invent a new *madeleine* for each 'act of memory', that is, an 'extrinsic occasion' of memory for each 'thematic unit' of the novel – Combray, Swann's Paris, Balbec and so on. Or rather, he would have been forced to envisage as many 'extrinsic occasions' capable of arousing as many memories in the 'I', in order to introduce each narrative sequence with a corresponding 'extrinsic memory occasion'. And in this way he would have effectively condemned his novel to develop as a sequence of scenes, each time engendered by an 'accidental occasion of memory', that is, as many *madeleines* for each memory-narrative. Thus we would not have had the *Recherche*, but rather a kind of huge tale with a 'replicated frame' (that is, the *madeleine*/occasion), along the lines of the *Thousand and One Nights*. Instead, the entire gestation of the novel, between the disappointments of the first attempts, with the *Jean Santeuil*, and the experiment of the *Contre Sainte-Beuve*, is ultimately a strenuous, increasingly conscious endeavour to avoid this compositional risk, that is, to avoid the memorial function being reduced to the role of a mere narrative frame – as happened, for instance, in Hofmannsthal's previous piece. In fact, in this case, the 'memorial frame' would have been continually reactivated, reproducing it from episode to episode, given the non-consequential nature of Proust's recollections.[49]

Theoretically, Proust had to make a choice: either multiply the narrative instances from the incipit, so as to produce a multiplicity of locutors (the different 'I'), or multiply the *madeleines*, so as to end up with the same narrating subject (the same 'I'), each time locutor of a different memory, provided by an 'external occasion' at the level of the frame.

We can note the tendency towards the first solution right from the first attempt in *Jean Santeuil*, although this novel is still narrated in the third person.[50]

Quelquefois en passant devant l'hôtel il se rappelait les jours de pluie où il emmenait jusque-là sa bonne, en pèlerinage. Mais il se les rappelait sans la mélancolie qu'il pensait alors devoir goûter un jour dans le sentiment de ne plus l'aimer.

[Sometimes when he passed their house, he remembered how often on rainy days he had dragged his nursemaid there, in his pilgrimages. But the memory produced in him none of the melancholy he once had thought he must inevitably feel when the day should come when he knew that he loved her no longer.][51]

A subject placed in a time x remembers himself in a past time x-1 ('he remembered how often on rainy days he had dragged his nursemaid ...'). But this memory, experienced in time x, is different from how the same subject, in time x-1, imagined he would one day remember it ('But the memory produced in him none of the melancholy *he once had thought* he must inevitably feel *when the day should come* ...'). This waiting for a future recollection ('when the day should come ...'), experienced in the past x-1 ('he once had thought ...'), actually prefigures a future $(x$-$1)$+ (... *un jour*). Moreover, this latter time $(x$-$1)$+ could virtually coincide with first time x (which is posterior to x-1), were it not for the fact that the two sensations – in x and in $(x$-$1)$+ – are different, leading to a gap or an ambiguity in their actual chronology. Indeed, the time x, that is, the time of the first diegetic statement, lacks the melancholy with which the future $(x$-$1)$+ was expected in time x-1. Therefore, we must admit that the two temporalities cannot coincide. We must admit that we have two different futures – time x as the future of time x-1 and time $(x$-$1)$+ as unaccomplished absolute future, without its own precise chronology.

Already at this stage of Proust's compositional project, we are confronted with a construction of temporality comparable to the times of the *ligne blanche* in *Sainte-Beuve* – towards which, between sleep and wakefulness, the sensations of the narrator and the two sick 'I's' are summoned. Both *Santeuil*'s and *Sainte-Beuve*'s pages produce, by the intersection of two different past temporalities, the sudden image of the future. In both texts, a similar arrangement of diegetic instances ensures that the future takes the form of an 'awaited memory', a recollection to come, which will re-happen. In the case of *Santeuil*, it occurs through the expectation of a future memory, when a subject imagines itself remembered by a later subject (... *qu'il pensait alors devoir gouter un jour* ...). In the case of *Sainte-Beuve*, it occurs through waiting for the return of the 'healthy time' in which the 'I' went to bed in the evening *(... un temps que j'espérais voir revenir [...] où j'entrais dans mon lit à dix heures du soir* ...).

The narrative space of the 'incipit in bed' – with its gradual attempts – is the textual place where these functions are tested. In the *Cahiers*, we can find other pages that show Proust's effort to try out every possibility provided by this type of incipit. Let us consider the following piece:[52]

> Je suis dans la chambre au château de XXXX < qui a appartenu autrefois à mes grands parents > où avant le dîner *qui n'était qu'à neuf heurs* je montais me reposer une seconde je me serai endormi, *on est* on doit être à table, on a peut-être fini de dîner. Mais on ne m'en voudra pas. Car bien des années ont passé depuis le moment où j'habitais chez mes grands parents. On ne dîne plus qu'à *dix* neuf heures, *en rentrant de* après la promenade pour laquelle nous partons à l'heure où *je rentrais* j'étais rentré depuis longtemps autrefois. [...]. C'était un plaisir quand on voyait le soleil couché mettre un bandeau rouge derrière le château, de se hâter pour trouver la lampe allumée et le dîner servi. C'en est aussi un, tout diffèrent, à ce même moment de se préparer à sortir, de traverser le village ...

Once more, a 'sleeping sequence' is used to break down the 'I', juxtaposing the different voices in a 'reversing-time'. The transitory moment of sleep is split into two different directions; along the diegesis, the sleep happens twice, yet always at the 'same time' – *à ce même moment*. Indeed, the 'same sleep' occurs, the first time, at a moment when the 'I' lived with his grandparents, falling asleep after a promenade, while waiting for dinner. Equally, the 'same sleep' re-happens, the second time, at a moment when the 'I' no longer lives with his grandparents and at the 'same time' – *à ce même momement* – is now ready to go out for other kinds of promenades. In the narrating mind and in the syntax, the time of this walk is in fact a place of transit between two ages. Within a single sentence, the 'same walk' is grammatically narrated as if it were happening at two different times: "... la promenade pour laquelle *nous partons à l'heure où j'étais rentré* depuis longtemps autrefois", 'the promenade for which we set off [now, *in the present*] at the hour when, once [*in the past*], I had already returned long ago'. Knowing which of the two walks is the diegetically 'ongoing' promenade – that of the present or that *d'autrefois* – would be quite irrelevant. Like *Sainte-Beuve*'s *ligne blanche*, like the future memory in *Santeuil*, this walk too produces a 'reversing-time'. The moment in which an 'anterior I' returns from the walk – to then fall asleep and wait for dinner – is the same moment in which a 'posterior I' prepares for the opposite action, that is, going out for a new walk, recovering from a sleep he had confused with that *d'autrefois* – when he used to sleep before dinner. The combination of the different instances produces a diegetic paradox: getting up a sleeper (*dormeur éveillé*). Or rather: letting an 'I' sleep, while another 'I' wakes up. In short, this is the main narrative outcome of the incipit as Proust uses it.

In the *Cahiers*, the scene we have just discussed – that is, the sleep in the *château* room – immediately precedes the narration of a mysterious stroll. Now, the narrator is accompanied by an anonymous *dame du château*. The promenade with this lady quickly alters into a dreamlike *peregrinatio*, as if it were an initiatory journey towards a landscape whose cartography exists only in dreams – "qui me semblait ne devoir se trouver que sur une carte du Rêve".[53] Thus, the sequence takes a dream-visionary form, which, later, the *Recherche* will reduce, to the advantage of the dream-memorial discourse. Moreover, the *dame du château* seems a Gothic hypostasis, a medieval *domina* that, in fact, foreshadows the Guermantes women[54] – as generous as she is demanding.

> la dame *jusque là* indifférente avait *tout d'un coup* un de ces mots par qui je m'apercevais <tout d'un coup placé à mon insu> dans sa vie à elle [...] d'où le lendemain du jour où je quittai le château elle m'aurait déjà fait sortir.[55]

Reading these sketches, the medievalist is reminded of similarly evanescent ladies widespread in courtly literature. For example, the seductive and reticent *dame* of the *Lai de l'ombre*: "or me fetes de vous partir, / sire – fet ele – ; c'estoit lait; / mes cuers ne me sueffre ne me lait / acorder en nule maniere; / por ce s'est oiseuse proiere" ['now, sir, let me depart from you, she says; it would be a disgrace; my heart neither allows nor bears that I consent in any way; / and therefore it is a useless prayer'].[56] But actually, this minimal medieval echo, rather than prompting comparisons with other female allegories found in thirteenth- and fourteenth-century literature, suggests a somewhat more systematic reflection. Let us attempt an evaluation of the Proustian *dormeur* in relation to the oneiric narrative of the medieval tradition. Indeed, the 'Gothic lady' would serve, in this sense, as an indicator of a broader textual memory.

3 The dreaming incipit (towards the *Rose*)

Therefore, if it is true that the Proustian 'incipit in bed' performs the structural functions we have just summarised, we might then attempt a comparison with the formal and narrative structures of the greatest 'novel in bed' of the Middle Ages, namely the *Roman de la rose*. As is well known, the *Rose* is the first-person narrative of an erotic dream, within which the voices of the 'dreaming I' and the 'dreamed I' are intertwined. It is interesting to note how these two monuments of Romance literature – that is, the *Recherche* and the *Rose* –, virtually the alpha and omega of European narrativity, deal, centuries apart, with a similar diegetic problem, leading to comparable solutions in their respective texts. Both novels face the multiplication of subjective instances and their coordination through the 'sleeping incipit' of the narrative. In our perspective, however, what is essential is not to establish the phylogeny of the sources, i.e. the (unlikely) hypothesis that Proust consciously retrieved narrative patterns present in the *Old French* novel; rather, it is relevant to compare the structural strategies shared by the two novels.

Dreaming the incipit 91

In general, critics have by now recognised Proust's medievalism, that is, the Romanesque and Gothic inspiration of his images: from the bell towers of Martinville to the Giottesque allegories of Swann, to the very conception of the novel as a 'cathedral'.[57] In this sense, the *Roman de la rose* is often evoked in studies on the 'medieval Proust', as many readers feel a veiled continuity between the two works. For instance, on the 'Proustian Middle Ages', we can read critical statements such as this:

> l'influence est certes celle de l'architecture des cathédrales, mais aussi des roses d'église, ce qui ne peut que faire penser au *Roman de la Rose* […], que Proust ne connaissait apparemment pas, mais avec lequel il partage de nombreux points communs: longueur, caractère encyclopédique enchâssé dans la trame romanesque au prix de nombreuses digressions, références aux miroirs et aux optiques pour définir le rôle du lecteur.[58]

Moreover, the historical epoch of the *Recherche* is the concluding season of an overall medievalism in European culture. Through the recovery, or invention, of a medieval imaginary, the nineteenth-century literature and arts had produced a sphere of narrative memory. In other words, the nineteenth-century medievalism produced a place of aesthetic estrangement or *rêverie*, as well as a fictional projection, particularly in France, of the *vieux pays*, of a *gauloise* infancy, as literary nostalgia.[59] Within that imaginary, the old country – ancient landscapes, medieval towers, abbeys and so on – and the young consciousness of novel characters overlap with each other. This inclination is evident in Nerval's work, especially in some pages that Proust knew well:

> des jeunes filles dansaient en rond sur la pelouse en chantant de vieux airs transmis par leurs mères, et d'un français si naturellement pur que l'on se sentait bien exister dans ce vieux pays du Valois, où, pendant plus de mille ans, a battu le cœur de la France. (*Sylvie*)

However, the comparison between the thirteenth-century *Rose* and Proust's novel firstly suggests another kind of analysis: not so much an evaluation of medievalism as a source of creative imagination – *à la Nerval* – but rather a level of pure 'synchronic' investigation. Indeed, I would like outline an enquiry on the diegetic

functions that both novels – six and a half centuries apart – activate in their incipit.
Let us start from the beginning of the medieval text. After a prologue on the veracity of dreams, the *Rose* develops its narrative incipit:

> Au vuintieme an de mon aage,
> ou point qu'amors prent peage
> des joenz gens, couchier m'aloie,
> une nuit si com je soloie,
> et me dormoie mout forment,
> si vi un songe en mon dormant
> (*Roman de la rose*, vv. 21–26)[60]

[In the twentieth year of my life, when Love asks young people to pay the toll, I went to bed one night as usual; I was sound asleep and in my sleep I saw a dream].

According to these verses, the *Rose*, that is, the 'sleeping novel' of a young man in love – his erotic vision and his obsessive search for the rose in the garden of Love – begins when the 'dreamer's I' was in his twenties. At that age, lying in bed one evening like any other, the narrative 'I' has a dream – the 'novelistic image' appears to him.

The age of 20 in the *Roman de la rose* – a typical chronology of the novel, somewhere between the expectations of adult life and the imperfection of one's desires – is the same age that reappears in Proust's sketches. In Proust, too, the age of 20 marks the phase in which the narrator splits into the couple of the sleeper and the narrative actor. It is at that age that the diegetic split of the subject takes place: the one who stays in bed and the one who acts.

> Jusque vers l'âge de vingt ans, je dormais toute la nuit avec de courts réveils. Quelquefois *ils duraient juste le temps qu'il fallait à mon esprit pour sortir de* mon esprit ne *faisait* sortait *de la nuit* du sommeil […] que le temps de le connaître et de le gouter < et < de décider > d'y rentrer au plus vite >.[61]

Therefore, the *Rose*'s dreamer is 20 years old, just as the Proustian *dormeur* is also 20 years old. But, in both novels, the most significant fact concerns the habitual and iterative nature of the temporality expressed by the twenties. Indeed, in the *Rose*, the diegetic iteration of 20 years' time is immediately made explicit, both through verbal tenses and syntagmas: "couchier *m'aloie*, / une nuit *si com je soloie*", '*I went* to bed one night *as usual*'. Thus, the 'bedtime' in which the novel begins occurs in the recursive time of the twenties, namely during its 'usual' nights. In the same way, the *âge de vingt ans* in Proust is nothing more than an intermediate variant along the several attempts at finding an incipit gradually leading to the discovery of the *longtemps*, that is, to the progressive identification of an extremely iterative time. Here are some 'genetic variants' of Proust's incipit:

Je venais de me coucher ...[62]
J'étais couché depuis une heure environ ...[63]
Depuis longtemps je ne dormais plus que le jour ...[64]
Quand j'étais jeune, je dormais la nuit ...[65]
Jusqu'à l'âge de vingt ans, je dormais toute la nuit ...[66]

From this perspective, the 'age of 20', marking the incipit of both novels, is not the 'singular time' of the adventure, of the 'unique' heroic action – as Lukács strictly understood it. On the contrary, the time of the incipit, both in the *Rose* and in Proust's sketches, is a habitual and recursive chronology. It represents throughout the diegesis a *during-time* – 'during the twenty years ...' – which resembles the 'long times' of the *Erec*'s *recreantise* ("sovant estoit midi passez ...") more than the times of the 'singular action'. Furthermore, in both cases the indefinite and prolonged quality of this incipit time is grammatically emphasised: like the *longtemps* of the *Recherche*, the *Rose*'s syntagma "si com je soloie" produces a diegetic iteration, that is, an indeterminate chronology that arouses in the reader the image of a sleep repeated in time.

Once this distance has been established between the act of novelistic enunciation – the time of the one who is narrating – and the iterative past of the incipit, the *Rose* produces further splits of subjects. Among these, the main one – and perhaps the one most akin to Proust's technique – concerns the 'reverse-time' that characterises the dream from which the novel is engendered. Indeed, as in Proust, the *Rose*'s subject, which unifies the different narrative instances, is a paradoxical *dormeur éveillé*. If in the *Recherche* and its sketches the 'reverse-time' emerges from the shifts between the various 'I's', which have been discussed above, in the *Rose* the 'reverse-time' emerges from the ambiguous diegetic instance: it is a subject who goes to bed at night and finds himself acting in the morning.

> Quant toute rien d'amer s'esfroie,
> sonjai un nuit que j'estoie.
> Lors m'iere avis en mon dormant
> que matins estoit duremant.
> De mon lit tantost me levai
> ...
>
> (vv. 85–89)[67]

[One night I dreamt that I was in that season when everything yearns for love *[in spring, in May]*. Then, as I slept, it seemed to me that it was already morning. Immediately I got out of bed ...]

With these verses the *Rose*'s oneiric *quête* begins. After the narrator has clarified the circumstances in which he happened to dream ('when I was in my twenties ...'), the novel seems almost to re-begin again, through a reprise of the dreamlike situation. Indeed, the sleeper dreams of waking up. That is, the one who has just gone to bed dreams of getting up. "Lors m'iere avis en mon dormant / que matins estoit duremant. / De mon lit tantost me levai", 'then, as I slept, it seemed to me that it was already morning. Immediately I got out of bed', which means, in effect, that the narrator initially dreamt of himself as a sleeper. That is, inside the dream he saw himself in bed and, while observing himself asleep, he woke up within the dream. In this way, the Old French novel duplicates the situation of the incipit; it doubles the content of the 'incipit in bed'. The latter recurs the first time in the prologue, at the outer boundary of the diegesis, in the *outside* of the authorial voice, when the narrator relates the antecedents of the narrative action – 'one evening, when I was twenty, going to bed, *I had the dream of which I shall speak*' – "or vueil cest songe rimoier" (v. 31). And then a second 'incipit in bed' recurs again *inside* the diegesis, inside the novel, when the singular plan of narrative action begins – 'while I was sleeping, *I dreamt that it was already morning and I got out of bed*'. The dreamer of the

Rose thus dreams of himself in the act of waking up. Here again, a 'Proustian reverse time' seems to be at stake: "une temporalité paradoxale: coucher à contretemps et anticipation du jour [...]. Le jour et la nuit ont échangé leurs valeurs".[68] The fact that the *Rose*'s 'dreamed I' wakes up and gets out of bed, remaining within the dream frame,[69] retrospectively means that the 'dreaming I' has dreamed himself not sleeping, that is, the dreamer dreams of insomnia. In this way, a mirror-image opposition is engendered between the dreamer who goes to bed at night and the dreamed-of who imagines it is morning and wakes up. From this point of view, the 'Proustian reverse temporality' could reverberate on the overall reading of the medieval novel.

In order to better understand the analogy with the incipit of the *Recherche*, we must recall the particular issue concerning the authorial status of the *Rose*. In fact, as is well known, the text of the *Roman de la rose* is transmitted by the manuscripts in a very ambiguous authorial form. A first part of the work – just over 4,000 lines – is ascribed to a poet, Guillaume de Lorris, who is said to have left the plot and the work unfinished. Thus, the second part of the novel would only be completed several years later – with about 18,000 more lines – by another poet, Jean de Meung, who names himself as the continuer and mentions Guillaume de Lorris as the initiator of the novel. That being said, one of the various pragmatic-textual arguments supporting the hypothesis that Guillaume did not finish his novel, leaving it 'without an ending', is precisely the apparently incomplete handling of the dream frame. In fact, not only in the part traditionally ascribed to Guillaume does the rose, that is, the object of erotic desire, remain precluded to the lover – when in fact the narrator on several occasions had promised its possession –, but the dream frame itself remains unsettled. Indeed, the first 4,000 lines end without the dreamer's awakening – which is an almost inevitable conclusion for a medieval dream narrative.[70] In fact, what is usually known as 'Guillaume's section' ends with the episode of the 'dreamed I' who, in front of the walls that enclose the rose, laments the imprisonment of his beloved and suffers for not having possessed her. Hence, there is no mention of the end of the dream in those 'final' verses. Ultimately, on a structural level, this means that the dreamer's narrative voice remains pending. That is, it seems that the narrator/dreamer would continue to sleep beyond the supposed end of the novel.

Such 'diegetic gaps' may have made medieval readers desire a continuation: both Jean de Meung's very long continuation and the other very short one in which an anonymous writer extends the narrative part ascribed to Guillaume by a few lines. In both cases – albeit with completely different poetic intentions – the structural objective of the continuation is to complete the 'logic' of the diegesis, that is, to make the 'dreamed I' possess the rose and to awaken, at the level of the frame, the 'dreaming I'. Here is how the anonymous writer of the short continuation solves this problem:[71]

Dame biautez en recelee
le douz bouton m'a presenté,
et je le pris de volonté
si en fis ausis con du mien
[...]
S'an revont tout celeement.
Atant m'en part et pren congié
C'est li songes que j'ai songié.

[Aside, lady Beauty offered me the bud; I gladly took it and made it mine. [...] They all left in secret, and I also left and took my leave. This is the dream I had.]

By such textual additions, we can infer that the possession of the rose's bud, that is, the oneiric fulfilment of the sexual act, foreshadowed by the diegesis, and the dreamer's awakening, that is, the dissolution of the oneiric frame (*li songes que j'ai songié*), represented for the medieval continuers the two narrative moves necessary for an admissible conclusion of the *roman*. However, what matters now, for our comparative purpose, is to observe how, in both the *Rose* and the *Recherche*, a complex, multiple temporality arises – which pivots on the 'sleeping' state of the narrative instance.

After all, regardless of the authorial and compositional issue,[72] there is at least one other place in the *Rose* where the text again duplicates the 'incipit in bed'. It is the encounter episode between the God of Love and the 'dreamed I'. Indeed, when the protagonist, in his search for the rose, personally encounters the God of Love, the latter teaches him the principles of the 'erotic art' and prophesies to him his future life as a lover. Among his erotic teachings, the God of Love prophesies to the 'dreamed I' that, as a lover, he will go to bed troubled by his desire for the rose and fall into a state between insomnia and dream, until, desperately waiting for morning, he gets out of bed and sets out in search of the object of his love. Ultimately, this means that the God of Love ends up announcing to the 'dreamed I' what is already actually happening in the novel – both to the dreamed-of and to the dreamer. That is to say, the God of Love – through the diegetic development itself – retrospectively announces the dreamlike situation of the novel's incipit: what has in fact already happened in the incipit – that is, the character's sleep, erotic dream and awakening – is (re-)announced through the speech of the God of Love as something that has yet to happen. Here is the divine prophecy:[73]

> Quant ce vendra qu'il sera nuiz,
> lors avras plus de .m. anuiz:
> tu te coucheras en ton lit,
> ou tu n'avras point de deduit,
> car quant tu cuideras dormir
> tu commenceras a fremir,
> a tressaillir, a demener,
> sor coste t'estovra torner
> [...]
> Tieus fois sera qu'il t'iert avis
> que tu avras cele au cler vis
> entre tes braz trestoute nue,
> aussint con s'ele fust devenue
> dou tout t'amie et ta compaigne.
> [...]
> Lors commenceras a plorer
> et diras: "Dieus, ai ge songie?
> [...]
> Dieus! Quant sera il ajorne?
> Trop ai en ce lit sejorne"
> [...]
> La nuit ainssi te contenras
> et de repos petit panras,
> se j'onques mal d'amer quenui;
> et quant tu ne porras l'anui
> soffrir en ton lit de veiller,

lors t'estovra apareillier,
vestir, chaucier et atorner
ainz que tu voies ajorner
...
               (vv. 2421–2510)

[When night comes, you will have more than a thousand torments: you will lie down in your bed, where you will find no quiet, for when you think you are asleep, you will begin to tremble, to wince and fidget, you will be forced to turn on your side [...]. Sometimes you will dream of your fair-faced beloved all naked in your arms, as if she had become your lover and partner [...]. Then you will begin to cry and say: "My God, did I dream? [...] God! When will the morning come? I have been in this bed too long" [...]. You will spend the night like this and you will have little rest – if I know what lovesickness is. And when you can no longer bear to stay awake in your bed, then you will have to get dressed, put on your shoes and get ready before the morning comes ...].

As is evident, the speech of the God of Love grammatically projects into the future – *tu n'avras ... commenceras ... t'estovra* – what has actually already happened (past) or what is happening (present) in the novel. The mirroring between the two different narrative situations – that is, the incipit and the episode of the prophecy – is quite explicit in some details. If, on the one hand, the God announces that the lover, tormented by desire, will get up and get dressed before morning comes, on the other hand, the 'dreamed I', at the beginning of the narrative, 2,000 lines earlier, had already performed exactly the same actions. Just like Proust's *malade*, in the incipit of the *Rose* the lover dreams that morning has arrived, and so he will get up and dress: "Lors m'iere avis en mon dormant / que matins estoit duremant. / De mon lit tantost me levai / chauçai moi et mes mains lavai ..." (vv. 87–91). As we previously observed, the same narrative image is transfigured in Proust's sketches:

> la raie de lumière qui, sous la porte dans la chambre d'un hôtel inconnu, trompe le malade; dressé sur son lit par une crise cruelle qui l'a réveillé, il voit cette lumière sous la porte et se dit c'est le jour.[74]

On the basis of such considerations, the 'incipit in bed' in the *Rose* recurs at least three times: (1) when the 20-year-old dreamer/narrator lies in bed and has a dream from which he derives the plot of the novel; (2) when the 'dreamed I' wakes up within the narrator's dream; (3) in the future of the lover who, according to the prophecy of the God of Love, will go to bed, dream and wake up tormented by passion. This prophesied time – that is, the third temporality – seems to announce a diegetic future, or some events that should concern the character's story. But in reality it directly involves the narrator's time – the writing's future –, since the God's prophecy actually announces the 'extra-diegetic' events that, according to the *Rose*'s prologue, have led the narrator to write his novel. The past of the dreamer in his twenties – that is, the one who goes to bed and dreams of looking for the rose – thus coincides with the diegetic present of the 'dreamed I' – the one who gets out of bed to look for the rose. And both of these temporalities, through the prophecy of the God of Love, bounce back to the future, which virtually evokes the narrator's time: that is, the time of the fictional voice, which is effectively future and later than the dreamer's 20 years and the diegetic temporality of the 'dreamed I'.

At this point, one might ask: perhaps the narrator too – like a Proustian *dormeur* – is in bed, sleepless, since he too, just like the dreamer and the dreamed, is still waiting to possess the rose? It is in fact the narrator himself who reveals that for him, too, the rose is still something desired and expected in the future. Exactly like his 'diegetic avatars', the narrator claims that he is still waiting for a future fulfilment of his love: "la bele, que Dieus garise, / qui le guerredon *me rendra* / mielz que nule, *quant el voudra*", 'the Fair – may God protect her – who better than any other *will give me* the reward, *when she so will*' (vv. 3506–3508; italics added). 'When the Fair will give him the reward of love'; therefore, the narrator, outside the dreamlike diegesis, is still waiting to possess his beloved.

The risk of our reflections is that they too may seem to be aimed at arguing for a kind of completeness, a circular autonomy, of the *Rose* in the part ascribed to Guillaume de Lorris. But in reality, the purpose is rather to emphasise, from a purely synchronic perspective, how, in the case of the *Roman de la rose*, the 'authorial status' of the text produces a novelistic machine capable of establishing certain inner temporal correspondences – regardless of their historical causes (be they the author's intentions or the novel's incompleteness and subsequent continuation). Indeed, the same question recurs in a similar way in the surprising lines of the second part of the text, when the supposed 'second author', Jean de Meung, seems to unveil, through a new prophecy of the Love God, the astonishing genesis of the novel. The God states:

> Doit il commencier le rommant
> ou seront mis tuit mi commant;
> et jusques la le fourinira
> ou [...]
> Ci se reposera Guillaumes
> [...]
> Puis vendra Jehans Chopinel,
> au cuer jolif, au cors isnel,
> qui naistra sur Laire a Meun
> [...]
> Cist avra le rommant si chier
> qu'il le vorra parfenir
> se tans et lieus l'en peut venir.
> Car quant Guillaume cessera,
> Jehans le continuera
> aprés sa mort, que je ne mente,
> anz trespassez plus de .XL.
> (vv. 10553–10594)[75]

[He [Guillaume] must begin the novel in which all my commandments will be contained; and he will write it up to the point where [...]. Here Guillaume will interrupt his work [...]. Then will come Jean Chopinel, with a cheerful heart and a quick body, who will be born in Meung on the Loire [...]. He will take the novel to heart, so much so that he will want to finish it, if he can find the time and the place. And so, when Guillaume stops, Jean will continue it – I will not lie – forty years after his death].

According to this piece, Jean, the 'second author', through a new prophecy, states that the novel so far narrated has not yet been written – nor even actually begun by Guillaume de Lorris. "*Doit il commencier la rommant / ou seront mis tuit mi commant*", '*he must begin the novel* in which all my commandments will be contained'

(vv. 10553–10555). The God of Love – pronouncing this sentence too in the future tense – claims that Guillaume has yet to begin the novel that will contain all erotic teachings. Furthermore, the God prophesies that Guillaume will not be able to finish the work, as he will die having written only the first part – "et jusques la le fournira …" (v. 10555). Thus, according to this new prophecy, another poet, Jean de Meung, will have to be born to complete the novel, more than 40 years later: this second poet will be able to finish the text, which Guillaume had not yet begun (vv. 10569–10594). What we paradoxically deduce from these dizzying verses is that in reality, the novel we are reading has not yet been written.

Critics well know the logical difficulties of this piece, and, if we take them literally, they seem insoluble. Since the *Rose* is the first-person narration of a dream, this second prophecy of the novel ends up stating that a new subject, called Jean, will enter the dream of a previous subject, called Guillaume, when the latter has already been dead for more than 40 years.[76] Solely by dreaming the same dream as Guillaume, Jean will be able to conclude the oneiric adventure begun by Guillaume, until the moment of his awakening: "et qu'il soit jours et qu'il s'esveille", 'the morning comes and he awakes' (v. 10606). But, at this level of overlapping, who can wake up and come out of the dream? How is it possible for Guillaume, the first dreamer, who would have died in the meantime, to wake up? And should we think that Guillaume's dream – or at least one of the dream levels established in the incipit – will remain pending for 40 years, available to be continued, regardless of the dreaming-subject's death?[77]

Nevertheless, it is evident that these verses from the second part of the novel interact with those of the previous prophecy of the Love God in the first part. The first prophecy was able to push the diegesis towards the future through a paradoxical circularity with respect to the incipit. In his first speech, the God announced "tu te coucheras en ton lit". That is, what has already happened in the novel's incipit will happen again. In parallel, through the second prophecy, in the second part of the novel, the work itself, its writing – 'you will write the novel'[78] – is pushed towards the future. In both cases there is a reference to a 'time of the incipit', which is conceived as a future time: the time when the incipit will happen again and the time when the novel will begin.[79] By means of these correspondences, the *Rose*, in both its parts, seems to pursue a structural objective: to simulate that diegesis and writing are both ongoing events – not-finished and mutually conditioned. After all, the close correspondence between the diegesis of the story and the writing of the novel has been operating from the very beginning. For instance, at the end of 'Guillaume's part' of the *Rose*, the 'dreamed I' and the narrator almost seem to stand side by side; in front of the walls enclosing the rose, these two textual figures grieve over the imprisonment of the beloved (vv. 3994–3996).

Que ma joie et ma garison
est tout en lui et en la *rose*
qui est entre les murs *enclose*

[... my joy and salvation are all placed in him [Bel Accueil] and in the *rose*, which is *enclosed* within the walls]

The excruciating expectation of erotic conquest, that is, the oneiric possession of the *rose enclose* ('enclosed rose'), is expressed by the same rhymes – precisely *rose/enclose* – that, in the prologue to the text, already served to announce the writing of the novel, the very name of the book (vv. 34–38):

Et se nuls ne nule demande
commat je vueil que li romanz
soit apelez que je coumanz,
ce est li romanz de la *rose*,
ou l'art d'amours est toute *enclose*

[If someone – man or woman – asks me what I want the novel I am beginning to be called, it is the novel of the *rose*, where the whole art of love is *enclosed*]

The rose *enclose* (enclosed) within the walls – which is still to be conquered at the narrative level – and the Art of Love *enclose* within the book – which has just begun and therefore still to be written – display their mutual involvement. In both cases, the novel – be it the narrated diegesis (the conquest of the rose) or the book-object that contains it – is 'enclosed'. The novel is 'enclosed' between the *outside* of an authorial voice that can only name it as a project – *li romanz que je coumanz*, 'the novel that I begin' – and the *inside* of a narrative character ('I') who dreams on several occasions of achieving it. From this perspective, dreaming of starting a novel, that is, dreaming of its incipit, represents – compared to previous examples (de Musset's *milliers d'enfants*, Balzac's Stanhope …) – an attempt to make the text, as in Proust, an "anticipation du jour". Ultimately, 'dreaming the incipit' is the attempt to keep the work in the fictional 'nocturnal time' of its project – before the morning really comes, that is, the time when the work-writing and the workbook will be irretrievably disjointed.

Notes

1 Del Lungo 2003, 34–38.
2 Ibid., 24.
3 Balzac, *Illusions perdues*, 65.
4 Balzac, *Les Employés*, 35–36.
5 Obviously, we are referring to the 'reality effect' discussed by Barthes (1989a).
6 The fact that in *Les Employés* Balzac uses the novel as a hypothesis on reality also appears in those pages in which, through the Rabourdin character, the narrator proposes a 'real' reform of the French public administration.
7 Genette 1972, 145–181. See the discussion of these notions in Chatelain 1986, Cariboni Killander 2007.
8 Lukács 1971, 97.
9 In the perspective of medieval literature, see de Carné 2016.
10 See Poirion 1988.
11 See Haidu 1983, Bruckner 1980.
12 Lukács 1971, 99.
13 Ibid., 112.
14 Genette 1972, 148.
15 Ibid., 149.
16 See Fusillo 2019.
17 See Herman 2018.
18 Foerster 1912, 11.
19 "Raconter *n* fois ce qui s'est passé *n* fois […]. Ce type anaphorique reste en fait singulatif […], puisque les répétitions du récit ne font qu'y répondre […] aux répétitions de l'histoire", Genette 1972, 146. Some medieval narrators seem to be aware of the structural problem linked to the repetition of diegetic facts. Chrétien de Troyes, for instance, when Erec has to narrate to Arthur all the adventures he has

undergone, wonders whether it makes sense to repeat to the reader – through Erec's account to Arthur – the complete sequence of actions that the same reader has already learnt from the narrative diegesis. "Erec a comancié son conte, / ses avantures li reconte, / que nule n'an i antroblie. / Cuidiez vos or que je vos die / queus achoisons le fist movoir? / Naie; que bien savez le voir" (*Erec et Enide*, vv. 6475–6480), 'Erec has begun his narration, he recounts his adventures and leaves none out. Do you think I will now tell you under what circumstances he left? Absolutely not, since you already know'.
20 Lee 2006, 69.
21 Hult 2009, 182.
22 Above all, I refer to the time of the liturgical calendar, in whose repetition the knights recursively await a call to adventure: "Et dit qu'a une Ascenssion / li rois Artus cort ot tenue" (*Charrette*, vv. 30–31), "tint court si riche comme rois / cele feste qui tant couste / c'on doit nommer Penthecouste" (*Yvain*, vv. 4–6).
23 Proust, *Du côté de chez Swann*, 13.
24 The bibliography is very extensive; on the dream topos in medieval French narrative, see Corbellari 2007, Badel 1980, Marchello-Nizia 1985, Demaules 2010, 2021.
25 See the "*topoi* du début", in Del Lungo 2003, 80–102.
26 Hamsun, *Hunger*, 1.
27 Hofmannsthal, *Andreas*, 22
28 Perec 1997, 16.
29 Ibid.
30 Barthes 1989b, 277–290.
31 Ibid., 282; italics in original.
32 Ibid., 280.
33 See Bacherlard 1971, 6: "a consciousness which diminishes, which goes to sleep, a consciousness which daydreams (*rêvasse*) is no longer a consciousness".
34 See Brun 1982. In the perspective of 'textual variants', see Lavault 2013.
35 In addition to the studies cited in the previous footnote, see Quémar 1976, 1978.
36 Brun 1982, 266. We transcribe the pieces from Proust's drafts according to the genetic edition of the *cahiers*: thus, the 'variants' and the different stages of writing are integrated into the text in italics. Given the complex, layered nature of these texts, we do not translate them.
37 Ibid., 244.
38 "moins triste que la raie de lumière qui, sous la porte dans la chambre d'un hôtel inconnu, trompe le malade", 'less sad than the ray of light which, under the door in the room of an unknown hotel, deceives the sick person'.

39 "L'erreur du malade sert de transition provisoire entre le narrateur de la matinée et le dormeur éveillé dans la nuit", Brun 1982, 294.
40 Ibid., 290.
41 Ibid., 247.
42 See Barthes 2015, 36.
43 Pinter 1978.
44 Ibid., 16.
45 Ibid., 17.
46 Ibid., 23.
47 Ibid., 115–116.
48 Brun 1982, 304–305.
49 In the novel and *Cahiers*, we can observe some traces of this 'primordial arrangement' whereby the narrator would find each time a 'pretext of memorability' to start the novelistic episodes. For example, the episode of lilacs, which, from the earliest attempts in *Sainte-Beuve*, perform a function similar to the *madeleine*, that is, they provide an 'extrinsic occasion' that arouses a memory and consequently open up a new narrative unit: "c'était la tendre odeur de lilas. Elle venait à moi comme tous le jours, quand j'aillais jouer au parc situé hors de la ville", De Fallois 2019, 56.
50 Genette 1972, 81.
51 It is chapter VIII, 1 "Madame Marmet" of *Jean Santeuil*, Proust, *Jean Santeuil*, 496.
52 Brun 1982, 281–282; see also the *esquisses* in Proust, *Du côté de chez Swann*, 651; italics in original.
53 Brun 1982, 285.
54 See Lavault 2013.
55 Brun 1982, 285–286.
56 Limentani 1970, 56.
57 See in this regard the significant essays collected in Duavl, Lacassange (2015), which take up the studies of Bales (1975).
58 Frasseur 2015, 126.
59 See Fuksas 2020.
60 Strubel 1992, 42.
61 Brun 1982, 261–262.
62 Ibid., 242.
63 Ibid., 244.
64 Ibid., 252.
65 Ibid., 259.
66 Ibid., 261.
67 Strubel 1992, 46.
68 Brun 1982, 290.
69 See Wright 1982.
70 See Badel 1980, 336; 2017, 303.

71 Strubel 1992, 240–242.
72 The authorial issue and the assumptions about the incompleteness of the first part of the *Rose* constitute an extremely complex philological problem, which cannot be addressed here. See the recent critical discussion by Badel (2017) and a number of studies that have tested in various ways the hypothesis that the 'part of Guillaume de Lorris', albeit it remains an open-ended text, might have an 'inner completeness': in particular, Strubel 1984, Hult 1986, Stierle 2012. Furthermore, the issue of compositional unity of the *Roman de la Rose* concerns another kind of hypothesis: that in fact the sole author of the text is 'the second', Jean de Meung, who fictionalised – by the narrative invention of a first author (the so-called Guillaume de Lorris) – the 'editorial affair' of his own novel – see Rossi 2020.
73 Strubel 1992, 160–164.
74 Brun 1982, 244.
75 Strubel 1992, 564–566.
76 Recently, a similar narrative plan has been developed by Christopher Nolan in the film *Inception* (2010), which might deserve a comparative analysis with the structures of the *Rose*. A team of so-called extractors manage to enter the dreams of other subjects; within the dream, the 'extractors' make the subject-dreamed fall asleep again, so as to produce various levels of dream action, each time leaving the upper dream level open.
77 In passing, we note that in this hypothesis one might identify the so-called Averroism that some critics attribute to Jean de Meung. The dream existing independently of the individual dreamer may metaphorically correspond to the Potential Intellect that exists independently of the individual acts of intellection – according to Averroist doctrine. In other words, the dream survives the dreamer, just as the totality of the Intelligible Forms survives the single acts of intellection. Regarding the philosophical context of the *Rose*, see Morton 2018 and the studies collected in Morton, Nievergelt 2020.
78 "Cist avra le rommant si chier / qu'il le vorra parfenir".
79 See especially Strubel 1984.

References

G. Bachelard, *The Poetics of Reverie*, Boston, Beacon Press, 1971 [or. ed. Paris, Presse Universitaire de France, 1960].

P.Y. Badel, "Songes et apparitions", in Id., *Le Roman de la rose au XIVe siècle: étude de la réception de l'œuvre*, Genève, Droz, 1980, pp. 331–409.

P.Y. Badel, "Le *Roman de la Rose* de Guillaume de Lorris est-il achevé?", *Romania*, 135 (2017), pp. 285–312.

R. Bales, *Proust and the Middle Ages*, Genève, Droz, 1975.
H. de Balzac, *Illusions perdues*, ed. J. Noiray, Paris, Gallimard, 2013.
H. de Balzac, *Les Employés*, ed. A.M. Meininger, Paris, Gallimard, 1985.
R. Barthes, "The Reality Effect", in Id., *The Rustle of Language*, Berkley and Los Angeles, University of California Press, 1989a, pp. 141–148 [or. ed. *Communications*, 1968].
R. Barthes, "Longtemps, je me suis couché de bonne heure", in Id., *The Rustle of Language*, Berkley and Los Angeles, University of California Press, 1989b, 277–290. [or. ed. *Inédits du Collège de France*, 1982].
R. Barthes, *La préparation du roman. Cours au Collège de France (1978–1979 et 1979–1980)*, Paris, Seuil, 2015.
M.T. Bruckner, "Repetition and Variation in Twelfth-Century French Romance", in *The Expansion and Transformations of Courtly Literature*, ed. N.B. Smith, J.T. Snow, Athens, University of Georgia Press, 1980, pp. 101–114.
B. Brun, "*Le dormeur éveillé. Genèse d'un roman de la mémoire*", in *Cahiers Marcel Proust*, 11, *Études proustiennes*, IV, Paris, Gallimard, 1982, pp. 242–316.
C. Cariboni Killander, "La théorie de l'itératif au banc d'essai du lecteur", *Poétique*, 150 (2007), pp. 239–255.
D. Chatelain, "Frontières de l'itératif", *Poétique*, 65 (1986), pp. 111–124.
A. Corbellari, "Pour une étude générique et synthétique du récit de rêve dans la littérature française médiévale", in *Le rêve médiéval*, ed. A. Corbellari, J.Y. Tilliette, Genève, Droz, 2007 pp. 53–71.
D. de Carné, "Appliquer la *Théorie du roman* avant *Don Quichotte*. Le Moyen Âge et ses 'vastes contes de fées'", *Romanesques*, 8 (2016), pp. 215–229.
B. de Fallois (ed.), *Contre Sainte-Beuve*, by M. Proust, Paris, Gallimard, 2019 [or. ed. Paris, Gallimard, 1954].
A. Del Lungo, *L'incipit romanesque*, Paris, Seuil, 2003.
M. Demaules, *La corne et l'ivoire: étude sur le récit de rêve dans la littérature romanesque des XIIe et XIIIe siècles*, Paris, Champion, 2010.
M. Demaules, "Le songe-cadre à la première personne: un format multivalent?", in *Medieval Forms of First-Person Narration: A Potentially Universal Format*, ed. J. Cerquiglini-Toulet, K. Philipowski, B. Sasse, 'Villa Vigoni Talks', 8, 2021, pp. 157–178.
S. Duval, M. Lacassange (eds.), *Proust et les 'Moyen Âge'*, Paris, Hermann 2015.
W. Foerster (ed.), *Yvain (der Löwenritter)* von *Kristian von Troyes*, Halle, Niemeyer, 1912.
V. Frasseur, "Le Moyen Âge perdu du *Temps retrouvé*. Un bâti de mémoire", in *Proust et les 'Moyen Âge'*, ed. S. Duval, M. Lacassange, Paris, Hermann 2015, pp. 119–132.

P.A. Fuksas, "Il romanzo come Forma Patetica della Nostalgia", in *Un'invenzione romanza: il romanzo e le sue trasformazioni nelle letterature medievali e moderne*, Atti del VI seminario internazionale di studio (L'Aquila, 26–27 Novembre 2019), ed. L. Spetia [= *Spolia*, 2020], pp. 151–166.

M. Fusillo, "Hierarchies, Details, Fetishes: On Lukács' *Narrate or Describe?*", *Revue Internationale de Philosophie*, 73 (2019), pp. 181–198.

G. Genette, *Figures III*, Paris, Seuil, 1972.

P. Haidu, "The Episode as Semiotic Module in Twelfth-Century Romance", *Poetics Today*, 4 (1983), pp. 655–681.

K. Hamsun, *Hunger*, English translation by G. Egerton, London, Smithers, 1899.

J. Herman, "Le roman médiéval et les chemins de l'aventure", in *Une espèce de prédiction. Dire et imaginer l'avenir dans la fiction d'Ancien Régime*, ed. C. Bournonville, L. Charles, 2018, online: www.fabula.org/colloques/document5674.php.

H. von Hofmannsthal, *Andreas*, London, Pushkin Press, 1998.

D. F. Hult, *Self-fulling Prophecies. Readership and Authority in the First Roman de la Rose*, Cambridge, Cambridge University Press, 1986.

D.F. Hult (ed.), *La mort du roi Arthur*, Paris, Livre de poche, 2009.

M. Lavault, "Du côté de l'incipit de la *Recherche*: la genèse de la fiction selon Proust", *Genesis*, 36 (2013), pp. 91–104.

Ch. Lee (ed.), *Jaufre*, ed. Ch. Lee, Rome, Carocci, 2006.

A. Limentani (ed.), *L'immagine riflessa*, by Jean Renart, Torino, Einaudi, 1970.

G. Lukács, *The Theory of the Novel*, London, Merlin Press, 1971 [ed. or. Berlin, Cassirer, 1920].

C. Marchello-Nizia, "La rhétorique des songes et le songe comme rhétorique dans la littérature française médiévale", in *I sogni nel Medioevo*, ed. T. Gregory, Roma, Edizioni dell'Ateneo, 1985, pp. 245–260.

J. Morton, *The Roman de la Rose in its Philosophical Context. Art, Nature and Ethics*, Oxford, Oxford University Press, 2018.

J. Morton, M. Nievergelt (eds.), *The Roman de la Rose and Thirteenth Century Thought*, Cambridge, Cambridge University Press, 2020.

G. Perec, "The Bed", in Id., *Species of Spaces and Other Pieces*, London, Penguin, 1997 [ed. or. Paris, Galilée, 1974].

H. Pinter, *The Proust Screenplay*, London, Methuen, 1978.

D. Poirion, "Le roman d'aventure au Moyen Âge: étude d'esthétique littéraire", *Cahiers de l'Association internationale des études françaises*, 40 (1988), pp. 111–127.

M. Proust, *Du côté de chez Swann*, in *À la recherche du temps perdu*, ed. J.Y. Tadié, I, Paris, Gallimard, 1987.

M. Proust, *Jean Santeuil*, English tr. G. Hopkins, London, Weidenfeld-Nicolson, 1955.

C. Quémar, "Autour de trois avant-textes de l'Ouverture de la *Recherche*. Nouvelles approches des problèmes du *Contre Sainte-Beuve*", *Bulletin d'informations proustiennes*, 3 (1976), pp. 7–22.

C. Quémar, "De l'essai sur Sainte-Beuve au futur roman: quelques aspects du projet proustien à la lumières des avant-textes", *Bulletin d'informations proustiennes*, 8 (1978), pp. 7–11.

L. Rossi, "Metalepsis and Allegory: The Unity of the Roman", in *The Roman de la Rose and Thirteenth Century Thought*, ed. J. Morton, M. Nievergelt, Cambridge, Cambridge University Press, 2020, pp. 201–231.

K. Stierle, "Le *Roman de la Rose* de Guillaume de Lorris est-il un fragment?", *Zeitschrift für französische Sprache und Literatur*, 122 (2012), pp. 259–277.

A. Strubel, "Écriture du songe et mise en œuvre de la 'senefiance' dans le *Roman de la Rose* de Guillaume de Lorris", in *Études sur le Roman de la Rose*, ed. J. Dufournet, Genève, Slatkine, 1984, pp. 145–179.

A. Strubel (ed.), *Le roman de la rose*, by Guillaume de Lorris, Jean de Meung, Paris, Livre de poche, 1992.

T.D. Wright, "Le cadre du rêve dans le *Roman de la Rose*", *Chimères*, 15 (1982), pp. 43–53.

Index

Aeneid viii, 10, 11, 13, 14, 20, 21, 24, 25, 30, 31
Aeschylus 41
À la recherche du temps perdu viii, 6, 7, 38, 62, 79–81, 83–6, 89–91, 93, 95, 96
Albert Savarus 43, 46
Anderson, W. S. 32
Antonelli, R. 62
Aristotle 2, 13, 31, 42, 51, 31
Auerbach, E. ix, 42, 44, 63
Azzam, W. 32, 62

Bachelard, G. 104
Badel, P. Y. 104, 105
Bales, R. 105
Balzac (de), H. 22, 43, 46, 50, 63, 68, 70, 79, 103
Barbiellini Amidei, B. 32
Barthes, R. 17, 32, 40, 49, 56, 62–4, 80, 103–5
Beckmann, G. A. 32
Bel inconnu 44, 46, 48, 49, 55, 63
Berthelot, A. 32
Blanchot, M. 49, 63
Boethius 13
Boiron, F. 63
Breuer, H. 64
Brun, B. 104–6
Brut 39, 40
Busby, K. 62
Butor, M. 63

Cahiers (M. Proust) 81–5, 88, 89, 105

Cariboni Killander, C. 103
Carné (de), D. 103
Cepraga, D. 13, 31, 32
Cervantes (de), M. 36, 37
Chase, C. J. 32
Chatelain, D. 103
Chrétien de Troyes vii, viii, 2, 3, 6–10, 13–18, 20–5, 28–31, 33, 36, 39, 40, 63, 73, 74, 103
Cicero 1
Cligès 7, 8, 32, 36, 68
Collet, O. 32, 62
Collins, F. 31
Colonna, D. 31
Contre Sainte-Beuve 64, 81, 84, 86, 88, 89, 105
Corbellari, A. 104
Cristal et Clarie 57, 58, 61, 64
Curtius, E. R. ix

D'Agostino, A. 31
D'Amour 58, 59
Dante Alighieri 37
De Fallois, B. 105
Del Lungo, A. 63, 104
Demaules, M. 104
De Musset, A. 50, 53–6, 63, 103
Don Quixote 36
Duavl, S. 105

Eco, U. 6, 31
Erec et Enide vii, 2–4, 7, 13, 17, 20, 22, 29, 36, 63, 73, 74, 93, 104
Escola, M. 64
Estoire del Saint Graal, 51, 53, 64

Index

Flaubert, G. 37, 49, 72
Foehr-Janssens, Y. 32, 62
Foerster, W. 31, 32, 62, 103
Frappier, J. 14, 20, 32
Frasseur, V. 105
Fuksas, A. P. ix, 62–4, 105
Furetière, A. 37, 52, 53, 62
Fusillo, M. 103

Genette, G. 6, 31, 44, 45, 62, 63, 70, 72–4, 103, 105
Gingras, F. 64
Guggenbühl, G. 64
Guillaume de Lorris 95, 96, 99–102, 106

Haidu, P. 63, 103
Hamsun, K. 76, 78, 79, 104
Herman, J. 103
Hofmannsthal (von), H. 77–9, 86, 104
Homer 41, 42
Horace 13
Hult, D. F. 104, 106

Illouz, J. N. 64
Illusions perdues 69

James, H. 46, 63
Janko, R. 31
Jaufre 74, 75
Jean de Meung, 95, 96, 100, 101, 106
Jean Santeuil 86–9, 105
Jerome St. 24

Kelly, D. 12, 32
Köhler, E. 32, 50, 51, 53, 63

Lacassange, M. 105
La confession d'un enfant du siècle 50, 53, 54, 61
La Duchesse de Langeais 50
Lai de l'ombre 90
Lanata, G. 62
Lancelot 51, 55, 75
Lausberg, H. ix
Lavault, M. 104, 105

Lazzerini, L. 13, 32
Le chevalier au lion 73, 104
Le chevalier de la charrette 104
Lee, Ch. 104
Les Employés 69, 103
Limentani, A. 105
Looze (de), L. 63
Lukács, G. 71–3, 93, 103

Maddox, D. 31
Mainini, L. 32
Marceau, F. 63
Marchello-Nizia, C. 104
Martina, P. A. 62
Meneghetti, M. L. 32
Mora-Lebrun, F. 32
Morton, J. 106

Nerval (de), G. 55, 64, 76, 91
Nievergelt, M. 106
Nitze, W. A. 12, 31, 32
Nolan, C. 106

Paradisi, G. 31
Paris, G. 32
Paul St. 24
Payen, J. C. 63
Pellini, P. 63
Perec, G. 79, 104
Perugi, M. 33
Petrucci, A. 62
Pinter, H. 85, 86, 105
Poetics (Aristotle) 2, 56, 31
Poetics (Horace) 13
Poiron, D. 33, 103
Proust, M. viii, 38, 55, 64, 75, 79–82, 84–8, 91–3, 98, 103–5

Quémar, C. 104

Rand, E. K. 32
Renaut de Beaujeu 44, 46, 63
Robert de Blois 58
Roman bourgeois 37, 52, 53
Roman de la rose viii, 40, 90–6, 98, 99, 101, 102, 106
Roman d'Eneas 39, 40
Roman de Reinbert 57, 59, 61, 68

Roman de Troie 39, 40
Roncaglia, A. 31
Rossi, L. 106
Ryding, W. W. 32

Saint Alexis 25
Saussure (de), F. ix
Schulze-Busacker, E. 32
Segre, C. 33
Seguy, M. 64
Servius viii, 10–15, 17, 18, 22–4, 26, 32
Stendhal 37, 62
Stierle, K. 106
Strubel 105, 106
Sugden, R. 63
Sylvie 55, 64, 91

Terence 12
Thibaudet, A. 38, 62

Toniutti, G. 64
Tornoiment as dames de Paris 40
Trachsler, R. 62
Tractatus Coislinianus 1–3, 17, 31

Uitti, K. 31, 32

Villa, C. 12, 32
Virdis, M. 63
Virgil 10, 14, 15, 17, 18, 20, 22–4, 26, 29, 30

Walters, L. 62
White, H. 64
Woledge, B. 64
Wright, T. D. 105

Ziltener, W. 14, 20, 33

For Product Safety Concerns and Information please contact our EU representative GPSR@taylorandfrancis.com
Taylor & Francis Verlag GmbH, Kaufingerstraße 24, 80331 München, Germany

www.ingramcontent.com/pod-product-compliance
Lightning Source LLC
Chambersburg PA
CBHW051755230426
43670CB00012B/2293